HOW TO BECOME A MILLIONAIRE

HOW TO BECOME A MILLIONAIRE

IF A BLACK GUY CAN DO IT, SO CAN YOU!

PAUL ALLEYNE

How To Become a Millionaire: If A Black Guy Can Do It, So Can You!

For information, address:
WMLB Publishing
6575 West Loop South, Suite 500
Bellaire, TX 77401

Library of Congress Control Number: 2017908865

ISBN 978-0-9988683-0-1
ISBN 978-0-9988683-1-8 (e-book)

Printed in the United States of America

First Edition: October 2017

DEDICATION

To those who one day want to say to themselves that they are "living the dream."

TABLE OF CONTENTS

INTRODUCTION

OR: WHO IS THIS GUY? AND WHY SHOULD I LISTEN TO HIM?

When you saw the title of this book, you probably had a few questions: *Who is this Paul Alleyne guy? Is he really a millionaire? And why the self-deprecating tagline – what does being a black guy have to do with making money?*

So, first things first: My name is Paul Alleyne. Or Paul Alleyne, M.D., or *Dr.* Paul Alleyne if you want to get technical about it. And, for those of you who give a damn, my last name is one of those names that no one knows how to pronounce at first glance. Let me help you: It's a-*leen* (with a soft "a"). As in, "*A lean*, mean, fighting machine." I know that's terribly corny, but it's the best I could come up with in the last 40 years.

But I'm guessing that what you really want to know is this: Yes, I am a millionaire.

And, although you probably figured this out already, I am also a black guy. This is important because, statistically speaking, a "black guy" – even a college-educated black guy – is the least likely person in America (or the world) to become a millionaire (I'll get into just *how* unlikely in the next chapter).

Now, I'm not saying that becoming a millionaire is easy if you're Asian or Latino or white. It's not. Becoming a millionaire requires hard work and dedication, no matter who you are.

But I am saying that, if I could become a millionaire – even with the statistical deck stacked against me – you can too. I am so convinced of this that I left a high-paying job as a medical executive to write this book.[1] And if I can help even one person achieve a seven-figure net worth, I will feel as though I have succeeded in my mission.

This is not an autobiography in the traditional sense, and I must emphasize that the purpose of this book IS NOT for me to boast about my success. That said, much of what you'll read here is based on my own experiences.

I'll talk about my journey throughout this book, but the Cliff Notes version goes something like this: I grew up in Queens, New York, in a single-parent household. My mom valued education, discipline, and spirituality. From fourth grade on, I attended private Catholic schools because she didn't think the local public schools were very good, academically or morally. My mom was a nurse with a master's degree, so we weren't exactly destitute, but we lived in the inner city and would never have been considered well-off. And yes, finances (or lack thereof) were often a source of stress in our household.

In other words, I didn't come from money. I worked hard and got good grades. After high school, thanks to an attractive financial aid package that included loans, grants, and work study, I was able to attend a four-year university. From there, I went to medical school.[2]

1 Of course, this is easier to do when you're a millionaire. As a millionaire, I could afford to take time off from my job to pursue other interests.

2 Again, this was courtesy of more student loans. Sallie Mae, God bless her soul.

My education helped me secure a job as an ER physician.

At this point, you may be thinking, "Of *course* he's a millionaire. He's a doctor!" But before you give up and stop reading, you should probably know that doctors are terrible at managing their financial lives. Yes, they make a lot of money, comparatively speaking – but the overwhelming majority are *not millionaires.*

So I want to re-emphasize: My journey is unique to me. It represents just one path to wealth. And it's one of many. **Your path is unique to you, and it's important to me that you find it.** Maybe you went to private school like I did. Maybe you attended public school. Maybe you were home-schooled or have a GED. Maybe you have a graduate degree. Maybe you didn't attend high school or college at all. None of that matters. You don't have to come from a certain background or have a specific level of education. And you certainly don't have to be a doctor.

I wrote this book because I honestly believe that *anyone* can be a millionaire if they are willing to do the following:

1) **BE TEACHABLE.** How do you know if you're teachable or not? Here's a quick test: If you think you know sh*t, but don't have – or haven't done – sh*t, then guess what? *You don't know sh*t.* Please try to humble yourself and be willing to learn from people who are more successful than you.

2) **HAVE A GREAT WORK ETHIC.** Unfortunately, this is not something that can be taught. The passion for being productive and successful is the fire that will keep you going long after multiple failures, common sense, or laziness tell you it's time to slow down or quit.

3) **BE PERSISTENT AND RESILIENT—AND KNOW THE DIFFERENCE BETWEEN THE TWO.** You'll need to cultivate both of these qualities if you want to succeed in your journey. Persistence means never giving up; it means staying flexible and teachable. You keep trying until you make it. Resilience means the ability to emotionally cope with failure. Because you will fail. Maybe once or twice. Maybe 10 times. But no matter how many times you fail, you must be able to get back up and try again.

4) **TAKE FULL RESPONSIBILITY FOR YOUR LIFE.** Are you self-aware? In my opinion, developing self-awareness should be one of the goals of the human journey. Unfortunately, many people don't take the opportunity to reflect on why they are in their particular situation or why they may be perceived a certain way. I suggest that you quickly adopt a zero-excuse policy: No matter your financial standing at this time, you must accept that your past decisions have shaped the way your life looks today. To quote Stephen Covey, author of "The Seven Habits of Highly Successful People":

[You] are not a product of [your] circumstances. [You] are a product of [your] decisions.

And to quote Paul Alleyne:[3]

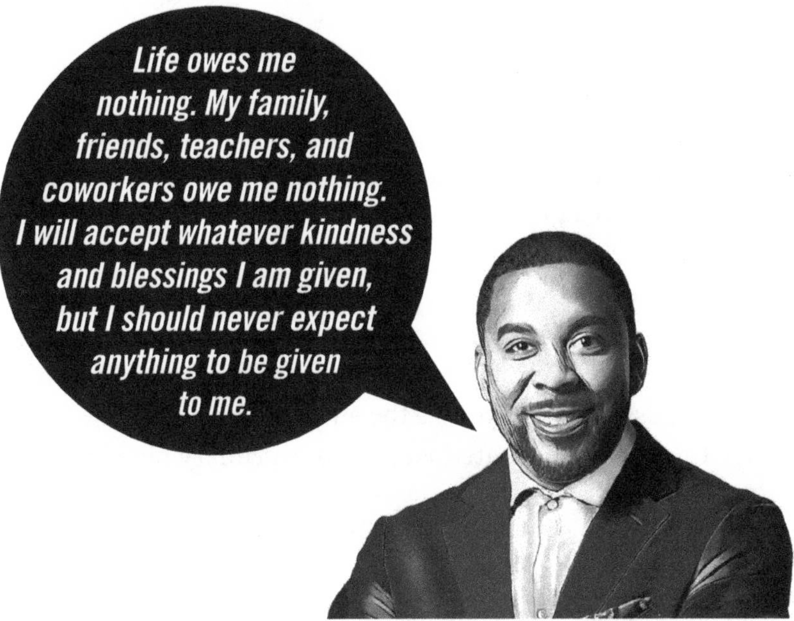

I came up with that as way to remind myself of the cold-hearted, painful truth contained in that statement. If you really want to become a millionaire, it will be up to you to make the right choices.

Before we go any further, I think I should make one thing very clear – if it's not already: **This is <u>not</u> your conventional personal finance book.**

I have taken the time to read almost every best-selling personal finance and/or investment book on the market in the last 20 years. What I found is that the majority of them just rehash the same concepts over and over.

3 And yes, I know that people who talk about themselves in the third person are pretty much universally viewed as a-holes. But it took me a while to come up with this, and, well, I'm kind of proud of it. But I promise this is the only time I'll refer to myself as "Paul Alleyne."

HOW TO BECOME A MILLIONAIRE

Do any of these sound familiar?

1) Live below your means
2) Save at least 10% of your annual salary
3) Have a three- to six-month emergency fund
4) Minimize your debt, especially bad debt like credit cards
5) Never lease a car or buy one new
6) Maintain a great credit score
7) Save for retirement
8) Save for college
9) Cut unnecessary daily expenses, like lattes or lottery tickets
10) Invest in a diversified stocks and bonds portfolio as early as possible to maximize the effect of compounding
11) Invest in real estate (usually your primary home with a 15-year mortgage)
12) Buy life, disability, and long-term care insurance

Most conventional finance books imply that if you do all of the above things – AND if everything goes according to plan – you will be "rich."

Here's the truth as I've experienced it: Following the rehashed, cookie-cutter financial advice above will definitely put you on better financial footing than most people. It's not bad advice. But it won't make you wealthy. It's not enough. Think about it for a minute: Did all the millionaires out there get rich by cutting back on their daily Starbucks consumption? Did Warren Buffet get where he is today because he stopped buying scratch-off cards?

Not a chance.

All of these books share one common flaw, in my opinion. They never ask you *THE* most fundamental question; *THE* question that you must answer in order for you to do any or all of the things they recommend.

It's a question so critical to your financial success that I decided to increase the font size so that it stands out both on the page – and in your mind.

THE question is:

HOW WILL YOU MAKE YOUR MONEY?

You need money to live. This is true regardless of your race, ethnicity, gender, religious beliefs (or lack thereof), sexual orientation, or political affiliation. You can work for it, borrow it, beg for it, marry for it, have sex for it, compete for it, gamble for it, or commit crime for it.

As an individual, you must accept the following unfortunate truth as soon as possible:

The amount of money you have or have access to affects the way you live.
More importantly:
The amount of money you have greatly determines the level of control you have over your life.

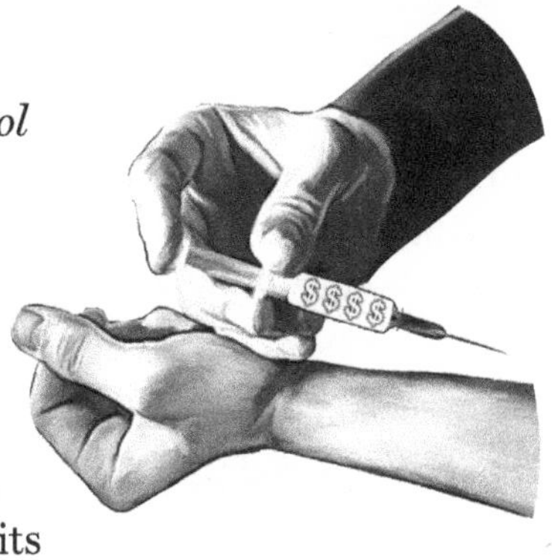

This is the reason why we are ALL in pursuit of money. This is why we fantasize about what our lives would look like if we hit the lottery. When we get money, it lifts our spirits (at least temporarily), but if we lose it or don't have as much as we need, we can become stressed, depressed, or physically ill.

The funny thing is, no matter how much money we have, there remains an undercurrent in each of us that always desires more. This probably makes money life's most addictive drug.

I know everyone has a different definition of "financial success." For the purposes of this book, I have defined financial success as being a millionaire. This means that you must have a minimum net worth of at least $1 million (not including the value of your primary home or retirement accounts).

But $1 million is just a start. Due to the decreased purchasing power of the dollar, $1 million doesn't go nearly as far as it used to. My hope is that, after reading this book AND applying the information contained within, you will exceed the million-dollar mark by several multiples. If you're bold enough to have lofty dreams, it's entirely possible that you'll reach billionaire status.

If you've seen the movie "The Matrix," you may remember the scene where Laurence Fishburne's character, Morpheus, gives Keanu Reeves' character, Neo, a choice between the red pill and the blue pill. If Neo takes the red pill, he "wakes up": all of the truths about life will be revealed to him – even the unpleasant or harsh ones. For the first time, he'll really understand the world around him. If he takes the blue pill, he'll stay in his dream world forever. He won't have to deal with the unpleasantness of reality, but he'll be living a lie – and he won't even know it.

So, take the red pill and come with me.

Nothing I tell you in the following chapters will be especially complicated. I wrote this book to be conversational and easy to follow. The challenge comes in taking the advice as you start your journey to wealth. That won't be easy – but if you do, I'm almost 100% certain that you will experience increased financial success and be on a more direct path to becoming a millionaire.

I just have a few final notes:

First of all, I sincerely apologize in advance for the profanity contained in this book. I went to Catholic school, and I come from a very religious family. That kind of language wasn't acceptable (and it still isn't). That said, sometimes, sh*t and f*ck are just the right words at the right time. So, I censored them to appease my family, and I left them in because I wanted the information in this book to keep it real.

Second, I have tried to keep this brief and remove unnecessary fluff. Most people no longer have the attention span to read books that are more than 100 pages unless it's about kinky sex, wizards, or vampires.

Lastly, please keep in mind that this book is far from conventional. But that's my intention, and all the words used (even the bad ones!) are 100% deliberate. Conventional thinking brings conventional results.

Who the f*ck wants *that*? Not me!

I hope you feel the same way.

Let's get started.

CHAPTER 1

THE ODDS, THE CHALLENGES, AND LEARNING TO SAY F*CK IT

This is Sisyphus:

You might recognize him from Greek mythology. Sisyphus was a king, and he was guilty of hubris, which, in his case, meant that he went around telling anyone who would listen how great and powerful he was, how he was smarter than everyone - even Zeus. And if you know anything about Greek mythology, you know that you don't f*ck with Zeus. Sisyphus learned this the hard way, when Zeus condemned him to spend the rest of eternity rolling a giant boulder up the side of a mountain.

This is where we get the word "Sisyphean," which we use to describe a task that seems endless, impossible, or fruitless.

For many people, the idea of becoming a millionaire seems like a Sisyphean effort. We feel that there are too many things holding us down; too many obstacles in our way. Some of us feel that we don't have the education or training necessary to become a millionaire. Some of us feel that our socioeconomic group, race, gender, age, or employment status makes it near-impossible to attain millionaire status.

It is true that some people will have an easier time becoming millionaires. If you were born into an upper-middle-class family and your parents, grandparents, and great-grandparents all went to college, you are more likely to become a millionaire. If you were born in, say, the United States or Canada instead of Haiti or Moldova, you are also more likely to have an easier time becoming a millionaire.

But it's also true that plenty of people from upper-middle-class families never attain millionaire status... while plenty of people from impoverished countries; lower-middle-class families; or less-privileged races, classes, or genders do become millionaires. In fact, these are the stories that tend to stick out in our minds.

It's not surprising when someone like Anderson Cooper or Paris Hilton becomes a millionaire. They are the children and grandchildren of tycoons, celebrities, socialites, and multi-millionaires. They grew up in a privileged world, and they no doubt entered adulthood with many more connections than the average person. Unless they turn out to be *complete* f*ck-ups, people like that are more or less guaranteed to be financially sound.

On the other hand, when someone like Steve Jobs or Mark Cuban makes it to the top of the financial ladder, we take notice.

They had to work a lot harder to get there. Although they didn't come from abject poverty, they did come from middle-class families and weren't born into money. The idea of becoming wealthy probably seemed Sisyphean to them – but they didn't let that stop them.

We all love stories about underdogs who overcome the odds to fulfill their dreams and/or destinies. Here are some examples from pop culture and real life:

- **DAVID VS. GOLIATH:** The little guy takes down the (much) bigger guy – with a slingshot.
- **THE MIRACLE ON ICE:** The underdog USA team beats perennial powerhouse Russia in the 1980 Winter Olympics Ice Hockey Tournament.
- **THE KARATE KID (THE ORIGINAL):** Daniel-san learns karate in a mind-boggling 90 days and beats up Johnny, an 80s bully archetype and Cobra Kai black belt.
- **ROCKY (ANY OF THE MOVIES):** The smaller, slower boxer beats up bigger, faster boxers after an intense musical training montage.
- **PRETTY WOMAN:** A Los Angeles prostitute meets a successful businessman; they fall in love, and he rescues her from her dead-end lifestyle.
- **LANCE ARMSTRONG:** This guy beats metastatic testicular cancer AND wins the Tour de France – seven times in a row.

The reason that stories like these resonate so strongly in our collective minds is because they feed into our belief in the human spirit and its ability to overcome adversity, even when the odds are stacked against us.

And let's face it. If we are being really honest with ourselves, we know how far-fetched a lot of these stories are. In real life, poor old Rocky would *never* have beaten Apollo Creed, Clubber Lang, or Ivan Drago. And Johnny would have literally put little Daniel-san in a body bag.

Even Lance Armstrong's story of beating the odds was too good be true: He eventually admitted to using performance-enhancing drugs, which certainly helps explain those seven Tour de France victories. People were mad about that, too – and I think our collective anger went beyond the simple fact that he cheated. I think what really pissed us off was that we need stories like his to make us feel inspired. We need people like Lance Armstrong to become the embodiment of hope, so we, too, can believe that it's possible to beat whatever Sisyphean odds we're up against.

We watched as Lance crossed finish line after finish line, and we thought to ourselves, "If Lance can do it, why can't I?" The truth, unfortunately, was that Lance *couldn't* do it. So he used drugs. Not exactly a fairy tale ending.

I'm not trying to be negative. I'm just saying that there's a reason why people like a good underdog story – but there's also a reason that they're called "underdog stories." Because of a combination of genetics, socioeconomic status, and plain old dumb luck, some of us are more likely than others to become world-renowned athletes or cancer survivors. The deck is not stacked equally, and the odds are not always in our favor.

So, what are the odds of you becoming a millionaire?

I concede that the odds don't necessarily determine your fate, but they do give you some insight into the likelihood of your desired outcome coming true.

Before I reveal the answer, let me share some of the odds of other relatable events.[4]

Your chances of:

> Being left-handed: 1 in 7.7 (male), 1 in 12.4 (female)
> Being homosexual: 1 in 43.5 (men), 1 in 76.9 (women)
> Being a vegetarian or vegan: 1 in 25
> Being 6'4" tall (if you're a man): 1 in 65.4
> Being 5'10" tall (if you're a woman): 1 in 41.7
> Not believing that there is a God: 1 in 43.5
> Getting a perfect SAT score: 1 in 5,152
> Getting into Harvard University (undergraduate): 1 in 13.9
> Majoring in business, management, or marketing: 1 in 4.9
> Majoring in communications or journalism: 1 in 28.8
> Majoring in economics: 1 in 104
> Having twins: 1 in 30.1, triplets: 1 in 723
> Being diagnosed with a mental disorder: 1 in 1.7
> Meeting the criteria for narcissistic personality disorder: 1 in 16.1
> Being hospitalized with appendicitis: 1 in 971 (men), 1 in 1,316 (women)
> Being involved in a plane crash: 1 in 3,128,000 annually
> Having O+ blood type: 1 in 2.6, AB- blood type: 1 in 100
> Being diagnosed with breast cancer: 1 in 8.1 (women), 1 in 769 (men)
> Dying of heart disease: 1 in 4.2
> Dying of cancer: 1 in 4.4
> Dying from an accident: 1 in 20.5
> Dying of Alzheimer's disease: 1 in 29.7
> Dying by firearm: 1 in 356
> Dying from suicide: 1 in 7.521
> Dying of the flu: 1 in 733,871
> Dying of the measles: 1 in 2,448,000

4 The statistics in this list are from "The Book of Odds" by Amram Shapiro.

Interesting stuff, right? Now, here are some other interesting numbers. According to a 2016 article in Bloomberg News, your chances of becoming a millionaire in America by retirement age – by race[5] – are:

Asian: 1 in 4.5
White: 1 in 5.3
Latino: 1 in 43.5
Black 1 in 52.6

The article goes on to say that receiving a college education can improve the odds a bit. With the benefit of an undergraduate degree, here are your chances of becoming a millionaire by middle age (by race):

Asian: 1 in 4.5
White: 1 in 4.6
Latino: 1 in 14.7
Black: 1 in 15.6

Your reaction to these odds will probably vary depending on your race and education level. As a black guy, I know that a 1 in 52.6 (or in my case, 1 in 15.6) isn't great. But at the same time, I don't view it as insurmountable. For one thing, I've always liked a good challenge. For another, I'm not sure just how accurate those statistics are. Those studies never tell you how many of those 52.6 (15.6) other people are *actively trying* to become millionaires. There's a difference.

I find it encouraging that I am still more likely to become a millionaire than I am to die in a car accident (1 in ~5,000), develop appendicitis (1 in 971), or be killed by a firearm (1 in 356 – a fate

5 Stilwell, Victoria. "What are Your Odds of Becoming a Millionaire?" Bloomberg.com. January 21, 2016.

too common for those who look like me and live in inner-city America). I also think it's interesting that the chances of becoming a millionaire are higher than knowing someone who is a vegetarian or vegan (1 in 25...feels like the odds should be higher since being either one is really trendy right now). It's also encouraging to know that the odds of me becoming a millionaire are higher than the odds of a man being 6'4" tall (1 in 65.4). Despite this being a relatively uncommon height, I have met plenty of men who are 6'4", or even taller, in my lifetime.[6]

In other words, I don't think that you should find the odds especially discouraging. It's a challenge, but it's not impossible. I did it – and remember that I'm a statistical underdog. So if I did it, so can you – *no matter who you are, and no matter what the numbers say about it.*[7]

At this point, you already know a little about me. You know my race, gender, education level, and chosen career. You also know that – despite the odds – I've achieved my goal of becoming a millionaire.

So, that's enough about me for a while. Let's talk about you.

Are you:

1) A man or a woman? A transgender man or woman?
2) White, Black, Asian, Latino, Native American, or multi-racial?
3) Heterosexual, homosexual, bisexual, or asexual?
4) A Christian, Muslim, Jew, Buddhist, or Hindu? An

6 This is particularly encouraging because the taller you go, the lower the odds. For example, the chances of a man being 6'5" are 1 in 122. The chances of a man being 6'6" are 1 in 513, and so on.

7 Again, all statistics in this paragraph are from "The Book of Odds" by Amram Shapiro.

Atheist?

5) A Democrat, Republican, Independent, Libertarian, Tea-Partier, Socialist, Communist, or a proud member of the I-Don't-Give-a-Damns?
6) Single, married, cohabiting, divorced, or widowed?
7) A child of a two-parent home? A single-parent home? Did you grow up with a foster parent, a step-parent, a teenage parent, or no parent at all?
8) From a supportive or an abusive home?
9) Healthy? Or do you suffer some level of physical/mental health issues and/or disabilities?
10) Someone society would consider an upstanding citizen? A criminal? A deviant?
11) A blue-collar, white-collar, or grey-collar worker?
12) A high school or college dropout?
13) A college graduate? An advanced degree graduate?
14) An introvert? An extrovert?

The interesting thing about these groups is that **THERE ARE MILLIONAIRES IN EACH AND EVERY ONE OF THEM**. I say this because I want to make it very clear that, when it comes to becoming a millionaire, your ethnicity, gender, religious preference, health status, level of education, sexual orientation, or personality type[8] DO NOT matter.

And in case you may be questioning my sanity or integrity after you read that last statement, please understand the following: Yes, I do live in the real world, and I do realize that who you are, what you look like, where you went to school, what family

8 For those of you who are into Myers-Briggs personality typing, I'm an INTJ, which stands for Introversion, iNtuition, Thinking, and Judgment. Like most INTJs, I'm fairly reserved and analytical, and I'm also independent, creative, and have a low tolerance for bullsh*t. Other INTJs: Michelle Obama, Arnold Schwarzenegger, Stephen Hawking, Jay-Z, Mark Zuckerberg, and, oddly enough, Lance Armstrong (which goes to show that the "judgment" component doesn't always mean *good* judgment).

you come from, and what you believe matter very much to some people.

I also know that being a member of a socially preferred group can put you at a greater advantage for achieving wealth than being a member of a group that has faced or continues to face challenges for equal treatment and opportunities. And I'm not just saying that based on my experience as a member of a minority group. There's plenty of research out there to back me up. This is why I added the tagline, "If a Black Guy Can Do It, So Can You!" to the title of this book.

Mind you, I'm not bringing this up to lecture you about economic inequality or complain about institutional racism. I just want you to understand how your identity changes the game. Note that I said "changes the game" – not "disqualifies you from playing the game." There's a difference.

That said, I will offer a word of caution to anyone who, like me, is part of a group that is statistically unlikely to become a millionaire: You'll need to bust your butt if you want to join this club. Trust me on this one.

But there's more to becoming a millionaire than busting your butt. There's one more piece of the puzzle; one more critical step you need to take before you start your journey to wealth.

What is it, you ask?

Here it is: If you want to become a millionaire, you will need to learn when to say:

F*CK IT.

Because in some cases, F*CK IT is the only proper response. Think that, as a minority, the odds are against you attaining millionaire status? F*CK IT. Think that, as a woman, you can't bust through the glass ceiling? F*CK IT. Feel insecure or inadequate because you don't have an impressive-sounding degree from an elite university? You guessed it: F*CK IT.

What is saying F*CK IT, exactly? It's learning to face the internal challenges and negative dialogues that hold you back and keep you from pursuing your dreams and achieving your goals.

The great 20th century philosopher/reggae artist Bob Marley[9] said it best:

What is the dialogue or story that plays in your mind each day? Is it positive or negative? Society and the media can beat you down and make you doubt yourself. Your family can discourage

9 Bob Marley was most likely an INFP, according to Meyers-Briggs personality typing. INFP stands for Introversion, iNtuition, Feeling, and Perception. INFPs are like INTJs with a slightly higher tolerance for bullsh*t. We'll discuss tolerating bullsh*t a little later in the book. Marley was also an avid smoker of ganja (marijuana). This may have also helped his tolerance level. LOL!

your ideas and dreams. The "experts" and "facts" may say that you probably won't make it.

Here's an example. As a black guy in America, I am:

A descendant of slaves
More likely to perform poorly in school
More likely to be raised by a single parent
More likely to be incarcerated
More likely to be a victim of homicide
More likely to be racially profiled
More likely to die in police custody
More likely to be unemployed
More likely to live in poverty
Least likely of any racial group to become a millionaire (even with a college degree)

It's not all bad, however. I am:

More likely to benefit from affirmative action
More likely to play professional sports
More likely to have a successful rap career[10]

Unfortunately, many of us take these challenges and stereotypes as "facts" about our respective backgrounds, using them to create negative dialogues in our minds.

What negative thoughts have been holding you back or shackling your mind from pursuing your financial goals?

10 I have always believed that a little self-deprecation is healthy. If you can't make fun of yourself and your circumstances on occasion, you miss out on both the humorous and tragic side of life.

Negative internal dialogues can lead to a feeling that we must work hard to desperately avoid: INSECURITY.

I believe in my heart that insecurity comes from those negative thoughts. We feel the need to be accepted; to conform to some ideal about what makes a person successful, worthy, attractive, intelligent – you name it. In my opinion, there are two types of insecurity. The first one is **SITUATIONAL INSECURITY.** A common example of this is the fear and anxiety that some people feel when asked to speak in public. Situational insecurity comes from a lack of experience and can be overcome with proper preparation and training. For example, you might be nervous the first time you speak in public. But you get through it. The next time, you're less nervous. Eventually, after you give enough speeches, you realize that it's not such a big deal.

The second, and more dangerous, type of insecurity is **CHARACTER INSECURITY**. People who experience character insecurity don't feel "good enough" about themselves and are, therefore, vulnerable to the opinions and criticisms of the outside world. Mind you, character insecurity (which usually begins in childhood) is not a sign of weakness, but rather a lack of confidence and/or maturity. These people often lack an internal barometer or the self-awareness to objectively evaluate their actions and decisions. Their self-esteem is based entirely on external factors. When everyone is pleased with them, they feel good. But negative feedback can make them become overly defensive, depressed, or disillusioned. This type of insecurity is much more difficult to overcome.

Sometimes this insecurity develops because you want to desperately fit in and not be seen as different. When I was a kid, I felt insecure about my last name. My friends all had last names like Johnson, Waterman, McLawrence, and Gillman. Names that were easy to pronounce and sounded just like they were spelled. Why couldn't I have a last name like that? Why couldn't my name be Paul *Allen* instead of Paul Alleyne? I remember sitting in class on the first day of school and waiting for the teacher to call my name, which he or she would inevitably mispronounce. Some kids called me Paul *ALIEN*.

Now, that might sound petty, but your name – and people's perceptions of your name – can have a pretty significant impact on your self-confidence and your potential future success.

Have you ever seen a movie starring Carlos Estevez, Demetria Guynes, or Neta-Lee Herschlag? What about a movie starring Charlie Sheen, Demi Moore, or Natalie Portman?

Would Bruno Mars' pop songs "Uptown Funk" or "24K Magic" have become mega-hits if he'd released them as Peter Gene Hernandez? Would the hip-hop single "Get Low" have had the same appeal if it was performed by Jonathan Smith[11] instead of his flashy, grill-sporting alter ego, Lil' Jon? Would Harry Potter have become a worldwide sensation if young boys knew J.K. Rowling was really Joanne Kathleen Rowling?

In some industries - like entertainment - your name is your brand; your key to success. If you want to make it big as an actor, model, or musician, your name can't be too "ethnic," too hard to remember, too difficult to pronounce, or too dull. In other industries, your name may even prevent you from even getting in the door. A research paper published by University of Chicago professor Marianne Bertrand and former MIT professor Sendhil Mullainathan found that job applicants with "very African-American sounding names" like Lakisha Washington or Jamal Jones didn't receive as many callbacks as applicants named Emily Walsh or Greg Baker.

Of course, names are easy enough to change. If your name is holding you back or making you feel insecure, you can do something about it. It costs money and requires some paperwork, but other than that, it's no big deal.

Other things are a bigger deal. Things that you can't or shouldn't change because they're a fundamental part of who you are. Things that make you different from most of the people around

11 We'll revisit "Get Low' in the next chapter. You probably know it, even if you don't think you do.

you. You may be the only woman in the boardroom. Or you could be the only Muslim kid in a school that's mostly full of Southern Baptists. Perhaps you're just one of a handful of gay or transgender people in your community.

This feeling of being the "other" is especially difficult in school, where kids are quick to pick up on little things that make you different. For example, when I was growing up, in addition to being the kid with the weird last name, I was also the kid who came to school in off-brand or entry-level Nike sneakers instead of Air Jordans.[12] You just weren't cool if you didn't have a pair of $100 sneakers. Today, it's all about technology – kids are quick to notice if their peers don't have the latest smartphone or newest, fastest laptop.

I can't count the number of times that I've been the only black person in a classroom, in a bar, at a party, or at a conference. I've had people make assumptions about me simply because I didn't look like everyone else in the room. If I were a different kind of person – more emotional, less analytical – this might bother me more than it does.

Here's a good example from the recent past: I was at a big professional development conference. It was an all-day thing that started with a breakfast buffet, and I was standing in line with a dozen or so other (mostly white) attendees. The guy in front of me turned around and said, "We seem to be out of spoons. Can you get some more from the back?"

I was wearing dress slacks and a button-down shirt, just like many of the other attendees. Hell, I was even wearing a name badge that said "Paul Alleyne, M.D." right there in big, bold

12 The funny thing is, now that I can afford to buy pretty much anything I want, I don't really care about impressing people.

letters. But this guy didn't notice any of that.

He saw a black guy, and he thought: *waitstaff.*

When I go shopping, I am often mistaken for an employee. I've been flagged down countless times by frustrated Target shoppers looking for price checks or rainchecks. I was not wearing the requisite red shirt and khakis any of these times. Go figure.

I think my favorite "only-black-guy-in-the-room" story is from a vacation that I took in the Caribbean. We were staying at a fairly upscale resort, and I was in the lobby waiting to check in with the registration desk when a guy asked me to carry his luggage to his room.

I told him that I didn't work there, and he was visibly embarrassed. Sometimes I think that I should have made him squirm just a little. Every now and then, I replay that incident in my mind, and I imagine taking his bags to his room, accepting a tip, and thanking him in an authentic Caribbean accent.[13] Later, I'd run into him at dinner or somewhere else and say, "Hi, Jim, How's it going?" in an American accent.

To be fair, I think that I was literally the only non-white guest at the resort, so I understand why he'd make that mistake. I might have thought the same thing, given the circumstances.

When I was younger, situations like this pissed me off or made me feel insecure. At this point in my life, though, it honestly doesn't bother me much. If anything, I find these incidents somewhat humorous. And I certainly don't let these interactions stop me from attending medical or educational conferences, shopping at

13 My family originates from the Caribbean (in fact, I'm a first-generation American). I can do a fairly spot-on accent.

Target, or going on vacation.

Insecurity about anything that makes you "different" - from your name to your sexual orientation to your race, gender, or religion - will prevent you from developing the courage to make bold decisions; decisions necessary to become a millionaire. If you are dealing with negative internal dialogues (or external assumptions) that are holding you back from financial success, you must get to a place where you are sick and tired of what's happening in your life.

You must learn to say F*CK IT.

I've found that, once I make this declaration in the face of a negative situation, I immediately become a new person. I no longer see the circumstance or the other person's opinion as an obstacle holding me back from a better future, but simply as another hurdle I must bust my butt to jump over.

Another thing that I struggle with is simply divulging the fact that I *am* a millionaire. This is not exactly something I advertise. I'm under the radar, so to speak. There's nothing about me that screams "millionaire." You hear those stories about people winning the lottery: After they win, all of these long-lost or new "friends"[14] and estranged family members come out of the woodwork. I wonder who will come out of the woodwork after I publish this book.

I was never a great English student. I know that there are a lot of people out there who got something out of reading James Joyce[15] and all that - but I was not one of them. I never felt that I

14 In chapter 14, we'll talk more about how your friends (and so-called friends) can help and hurt your journey to millionaire status.

15 I still suffer from post-traumatic stress from reading "Dubliners."

was especially good at writing, either. But my chosen profession actually requires a lot of writing – reports, emails, and presentations. I had to get over my insecurity and aversion. Eventually, I realized that my written communication skills were perfectly fine. And look at me now: I wrote a book! Of course, I still feel a bit insecure about it. My negative internal dialogue is a constant stream of: *What if it doesn't sell? What if nobody reads it? If it doesn't sell, does that mean I failed?*

And when those insecurities and questions pop up, I say F*CK IT. Lots of people have written books. Why not me? And if it doesn't sell? F*CK IT. I expressed something that was true to me – exactly as I wanted to say it. Deep down inside, I also felt as though I had a responsibility to share what I have learned with as many wannabe-millionaires as possible.

To quote Robert Herjavec from the television show "Shark Tank":

This is my humble attempt to impart said wisdom to you.

So, in summary: Identify what makes you insecure. Admit your weaknesses. Understand what keeps you in a state of mental slavery. And remember, you must be completely honest with yourself. You can BS your parents, spouse, friends, co-workers, etc. - but never BS yourself. Everyone has shortcomings and weaknesses. You need to understand yours. Know what you need to learn. **BE TEACHABLE.**

If you are serious about becoming a millionaire, I don't want you to spend too much time thinking about the things that make you different or the things that make you feel insecure.

Most people are so consumed with who they are that they never ask themselves the question that matters more than anything else. This is the question you will have to ask yourself time and time again as you progress through your journey of becoming wealthy.

It is THE question I ask myself almost every day, and I would like you to do the same.

We'll get to it in the next chapter.

CHAPTER 2

WHAT <u>CAN</u> YOU DO?

As a species, we have come up with a pretty obnoxious short cut to determine another person's skills. When you meet someone for the first time, how long does it take for them to ask:

"What do you do?"

On the surface, this is standard small talk. It's something people say when they don't really know what else to say. It's fairly harmless; it's not too personal. But people also use this information to make inferences about your intelligence, education, income, lifestyle, morals, etc. They also make inferences about the skills that you may or may not possess.

And we all do it. Everyone has biases, and we all make snap judgments about people based on all kinds of things, from race and gender to education and work.

What comes to your mind when I list the following professions?

- Manager at Walmart
- Used car salesperson

- Politician
- Elementary school teacher
- Professional athlete
- Investment banker
- White House intern
- Catholic priest
- Emergency physician

When you thought of the Walmart manager, did you imagine someone with a high school diploma? A college degree? A graduate degree? Did you imagine someone Muslim? Jewish?

What about the used car salesperson? I'm guessing that your gut reaction was somewhat negative. The stereotypical image of a used car salesperson is someone dishonest and maybe a little too pushy or eager to make a deal. Hell, in our culture, "used car salesman" has become a pejorative.

If you were a teenager or adult when the Bill Clinton/Monica Lewinsky affair happened, the words "White House intern" may still have a slightly unsavory connotation. If you were born in the 90s or later, on the other hand, "White House intern" might sound like a cool job.

And what do you envision when you think of a Catholic priest? Do you imagine a caring spiritual leader? Or a sexual predator?

When you think of an emergency physician, do you imagine a man or a woman? Do you picture someone white? Someone black? Someone Asian? Someone gay? Someone straight?

On countless shifts at the hospital, patients have assumed that I'm a nurse or maybe an X-ray tech or possibly a respiratory therapist. It simply never crosses their mind that I might be the doctor. This doesn't bother me. Maybe it's because I'm an INTJ and tend to be more analytical about things, but I don't think there's any malice or intentional racism behind the assumption that I'm a nurse or a tech. Besides, these are admirable jobs. I don't take it personally, and it doesn't offend me. I say F*CK IT, and I move on.

Our biases are based on our personal experiences and the result of a lifetime of conditioning. For many people – especially older folks or those living in the Deep South – the thought of a black doctor is still fairly new. They probably grew up going to white doctors. When they think "doctor," they do not picture someone who looks like me.[16]

Do biases make you a bad person? No. But you have to be honest with yourself about your own biases. You have to understand how your experiences and your conditioning have shaped your worldview, and then you have to police yourself and keep those biases in check.

This is important to remember as you begin your journey to millionaire status. All too often, people say to themselves:

> *"I can't become a millionaire because I'm a Walmart manager."*
> *"She can't be a millionaire. She sells cars."*
> *"He can't ever dream of having a million dollars. He's a biology teacher."*

And so on.

They're letting their biases – their ideas about what millionaires "do" – get in the way of their goal. The flip side is also true: Just

16 This happens often with female doctors, too – of any race. Ask any female doctor how often she's been called "Nurse."

because someone has a prestigious job title (doctor, lawyer, etc.) doesn't automatically mean that they are millionaires, either.

If you want to be a millionaire, the question goes beyond "What do you do?" The better question is, "What can you do? What are your marketable skills?"

For the purposes of this book, I define a "skill" as something you can do that the market believes is valuable.[17] In other words, it's something that people will pay you to do or provide for them.

There are a fortunate few out there who have been blessed with gifts of natural athleticism (Michael Jordan) or beauty (Heidi Klum and Halle Berry). Others may be computer science geniuses (Bill Gates and Mark Zuckerberg). Mind you, all of these people still busted their butts to get to where they are, but they were also fortunate to win the genetic DNA lottery.

The luckiest bastards of all are those who were born into wealth and therefore will never have the need to read a book like this one. The other 99.9% of us are born without any clear, income-producing skill.

But over time, through a combination of education, work, and life experience, we all acquire marketable skills. Not sure what your skill is? Think of it this way: If your boss or company is paying you for what you do, you have a marketable skill – no matter what your job title happens to be.

Here are a few examples:

- An NFL quarterback can throw a football pretty accurately, memorize the team's playbook, and read the

17 What the market believes is key. We'll talk more about this in Chapter 4.

opponent's defenses. He also has leadership skills, and he knows how to motivate and rally his team members when the game isn't going well.

- A computer programmer can write code that leads to the creation of new websites or software programs. But computer programmers also have to be capable of learning multiple computer languages, and they must be detail-oriented: One tiny mistake in the code can prevent the program from running.

- An emergency physician like me has the skill to diagnose, stabilize, and treat most of the acute medical and traumatic conditions that we encounter. Because we never know who is going to walk through the ER doors, we have to be able to communicate and empathize with a diverse range of people.

- A high school teacher possesses in-depth knowledge of an academic subject such as math, reading, or science. He or she also has the skill and patience to pass that knowledge on to students with vastly different skills, experiences, and learning styles.

- A plumber can repair, install, and design pipes and drainage systems. This requires not only physical skills, but a knowledge of math, the ability to read blueprints, and staying up-to-date with local building codes.

- A journalist has good written communication skills, but he or she also possesses the ability to research and process large amounts of new information, as well as the ability to observe and listen.

Before we move on, I want you to take a moment to think about your own skills. Fill in the blanks:

I AM A/AN ______________________________

____

____

MY SKILL IS ______________________________

____

____

Feeling stuck? I'll give you an example using one of the most common jobs in America: a retail salesperson. If I were in retail sales, my skill statement would go something like this:

I am a retail salesperson, and my skill is the ability to learn about and clearly communicate the benefits of the products I sell to my customers, and to sell those products in a genuine and personable way. I not only learn about my company's products, but know how to connect with my customers, as well.

If I were in retail sales, I would feel very proud to say that. That's exactly the set of skills that I would need to be good at my job.

Now, here's something you have to remember:

YOUR SKILLS ARE VERY DIFFERENT FROM YOUR KNOWLEDGE.

All too often, people confuse the two – and, like it or not, when it comes to accumulating wealth, only one really matters.

What's the difference between knowledge and skills? Here are some examples:

YOUR KNOWLEDGE	YOUR SKILL
You know all of the rules of baseball. You can recite all of the stats of your favorite players or teams.	You can throw a fastball at 100 MPH. You can hit a baseball 30% of the time. You are so good at these things that the market will pay you millions of dollars per year to do them.
You know all the words to "The Star-Spangled Banner."	You can sing "The Star-Spangled Banner" well enough that someone will pay you to perform it at the opening of a game like the Super Bowl.
You know the mechanics of how an airplane works.	You can fly an airplane or fix one.
You know all the ingredients to make a pretty tasty hamburger.	You can open a chain of restaurants and sell 1 million hamburgers per year.
You know the difference between freestyle, backstroke, breaststroke, and butterfly.	You can swim 100 meters or more using one or a combination of these strokes.
You know the difference between the Mona Lisa and Sistine Chapel.	You can paint like Leonardo da Vinci or Michelangelo.
You can recite Jack Nicholson's entire "You can't handle the truth" speech from the courtroom scene in the movie "A Few Good Men".	Your acting ability is as good or better than Jack Nicholson's.
You know the stock symbols for 20 of your favorite companies.	You can invest as successfully as Warren Buffet.

If you have even a passing knowledge of early-2000s American pop culture, you have probably heard the song "Get Low" by Lil Jon & The East Side Boyz.[18] Even if you don't know the song by name, you'll probably recognize the lyrics:

To the window, to the wall!
'Til the sweat drop down my balls
*'Til all these b*tches crawl*
*'Til all skeet skeet motherf*ckers . . .*

And so on.

You may think that "Get Low" is filthy, vulgar garbage with no artistic merit whatsoever.

Or you may think that it's a classic genre-defining example of Dirty South hip-hop. And if you do, you're definitely not alone: "Get Low" was a single from Lil Jon's "Kings of Crunk" album, which sold so well it went double platinum in 2003.

In other words, two million people found enough value in Lil Jon and "Get Low" that they paid to own a copy of his album. That song was everywhere for a while. Hell, you can even see Sandra Bullock dance around a campfire and sing it to Betty White in the 2009 romantic comedy "The Proposal."[19]

Speaking of sweat, I spent a significant portion of time in medical school learning all about glands. The human body possesses two types of glands: endocrine and exocrine. Endocrine glands

18 Lil Jon, by the way, is a multi-millionaire. Like every other multi-millionaire, he worked his butt off to get where he is. In addition to his music career, he is an actor and an entrepreneur (he launched his own wine label, Little Jonathan Winery, in 2008).

19 If you haven't seen this, I suggest you stop reading right now and Google "YouTube Sandra Bullock Get Low." It's worth it.

secrete their products directly into the bloodstream. The pancreas is an example of an endocrine gland.[20] It makes insulin, which is released into your bloodstream and is responsible for regulating your blood sugar levels. Exocrine glands secrete their products on surfaces outside of the bloodstream (it's a lot more complicated than that, but you get the point). Sweat glands are an example of exocrine glands.

To make matters more complicated, there are two types of sweat glands: Eccrine and apocrine. Eccrine sweat glands are located all over the body and produce the majority of what we know as sweat. Apocrine sweat glands are located in the armpits, groin, and anus area. They don't help us cool down but, when left unchecked, lead to the dreaded condition known as B.O. (body odor).

Again, this is a gross oversimplification of sweat glands. I don't remember now, but I probably put in an all-nighter or two to commit this information to memory.

If only I'd known that I could make a million dollars crafting a catchy song hook based on the material I was studying, substituting "testicles" for something colloquial like "balls" and putting that to a club-type beat.

To be honest, I probably would have messed it up by being too technical. "'Til the perspiration drop down my scrotum" just doesn't seem to have the same ring to it.[21]

Lil Jon may or may not know the biology behind perspiration – but that doesn't matter. To be a successful musician, you don't need to have a background in biology. You *do* need to have

20 For the medical folks and/or physiology sticklers out there: The pancreas is actually an endocrine AND an exocrine gland.

21 As an ER physician, I actually spend a fair amount of time thinking about balls. Of course, instead of sweat, I think about blood flow. Balls can get twisted and die due to lack of blood flow. But I doubt anyone would want to hear a song about that.

writing skills and an ear for catchy lyrics. You need to be comfortable on stage, performing in front of others. And you need to be able to market yourself – because nobody is just going to hand you a record contract.

The "knowledge-vs-skills" thing really hit home for me while I was watching an episode of the NFL reality show, "Hard Knocks." In this particular episode, one of the league's best and highest-paid players, J.J. Watt,[22] asked one of his teammates, Vince Wilfork, if he knew how to spell the word SPAGETTI.

"No," Vince said. He didn't miss a beat, and he didn't say it with even a hint of embarrassment.

And then J.J. said something that struck me as very profound:

22 Just to put "highest-paid" into context: Watt signed a $100 million contract with the Houston Texans in 2014.

Knowing how to spell SPAGETTI has no monetary value and therefore does not qualify as a skill, according to the definition in this book. The ability to "hit hard" and wreak havoc on the NFL offenses does.

Although I can properly spell "spaghetti,"[23] no one is going to pay me a lot of money to do that. In my professional life, I've come across several millionaires who have become wildly successful despite gaps in their ability to write, read, speak, and/or spell properly. Here are some examples of common things that would have driven my elementary Catholic school teachers crazy:

1) Sorry I'm late. Traffic was very heavy. I should of went the other way.

23 Admit it: You thought that I accidentally misspelled it at first and that my editor also failed to catch my error. But even if I actually thought it was spelled SPAGETTI, it probably wouldn't matter much, financially speaking. Like J.J. Watt, I have chosen a career path that does not require me to be good at spelling. Knowing how to spell makes me look smarter on paper, but it doesn't affect my ability to do my job as an ER physician or earn money.

2) Your outfit is beautiful. It's very sheik.
3) I hate it when my team looses.
4) Einstein's 3 Laws of Motion are the foundation of modern physics.
5) For all intensive purposes, people who leave the ER before being seen by a doctor should not count as patients.

If you don't see anything wrong with any of these sentences, don't worry. It won't limit your chances of becoming a millionaire. For those of you who care to appear more intelligent, let me point out the errors:

1) Improper grammar: I should have gone the other way.
2) Wrong homophone selected: Your outfit is very chic.
3) Spelling error: I hate it when my team loses.
4) Knowledge error: Isaac Newtown formulated the 3 Laws of Motion.
5) Syntax error: For all intents and purposes . . .

There are several other prevalent examples I could mention:

- Improper use of "there," "their," and "they're" or "your" and "you're" (more homophones)
- Improper use of "its" vs "it's" (the *'s* is NOT possessive)
- Use of "alot" instead of "a lot" ("a lot" is two words)
- "Africa is such a beautiful country!" (Africa is a continent)
- "You're from Ecuador? Where is that in Mexico relative to Cancun?" (Where do I start?)

Again – and I want to make this as clear as possible – when it comes to making serious money, none of this matters.

We spend our time in school learning a multitude of facts, and – I hate to say it – but most of this time is wasted. Don't get me wrong: Acquiring book knowledge is the first step in acquiring a set of marketable skills. But as someone who spent 20-plus years in the formal education system, I can confidently say the following:

Unless you are pursuing a career that requires adhering to a rigid track (e.g. doctor, lawyer, engineer, etc.), acquiring a large amount of facts is pretty useless, from a financial point of view.

Most of the facts we know have no financially rewarding application – although they do make us feel pretty good nevertheless.

Here's an example in my own life: I am a fan of the stock market.[24] Multiple times per day, I check to see how the market – and the stocks that I own – are performing. As a result of following the market for the past 15+ years, I have learned the stock trading symbol for mostly every relevant stock that trades today. Recently, I was on a conference call with a sales rep from Canada, and I asked her where she lived. She told me that she lived in a little city outside of Toronto.

"Which one?" I asked.

"Oh, you've probably never heard of it," she said. "It's called Waterloo."

"I know Waterloo," I said. "It's the home of Blackberry, formerly known as Research in Motion."

This sales rep was absolutely shocked and impressed that I knew this bit of trivia. I have to admit that – for about 30 seconds – I felt pretty damn proud that I'd managed to impress the hell out

24 I'll talk about the stock market later. Don't worry, though: I'm not going to tell you to buy stocks (that's conventional personal finance sh*t).

of this Canadian sales rep from Waterloo.

Knowing facts makes us feel good. We feel smart, especially if those around us don't know the answers (or if they don't expect us to know the answers).

Can you:

> Name all the "Brady Bunch" kids (oldest to youngest)?
> Recite Einstein's most famous equation?
> Name the Caribbean nation with the lowest suicide rate?
> State the square root of 625?[25]

Didn't you get a good feeling knowing some or all of the answers? Of course you did. It's the same feeling you get when you know the correct answers when playing along with TV games shows like "Jeopardy." However, unless you end up on a game show, knowing Marcia from Jan is not going to help you financially.

This is how I feel about the national spelling bees, too. Yes, winning is a great achievement – but what value is there in teaching kids to memorize the spelling of words no one ever uses, can't properly pronounce, and definitely can't define?

Here's a better idea: Teach your kid how to spell the word *millionaire.*

Hell, if you want them to learn what language the word originated from (French) and then have it used in a sentence ("A *millionaire* will have a better standard of living than most people"), feel free to do so.

---

25 For the geeks out there: Greg, Marcia, Peter, Jan, Bobby, and Cindy; E=mc2; Jamaica (could that be the ganja effect); 25

After that, please don't waste everyone's time learning how to spell words like *appoggiatura*[26] or *feuilleton.*[27]

Instead, put that time into developing marketable skills or creating something that other people will value enough to pay hard-earned money for. The song "Get Low" has become somewhat of an inspiration for me. Almost every day, I give myself the following challenge:

Can you create something as – or more – impactful than:
To the window, to the wall!
'Til the sweat drop down my balls?

And you know what? Somewhere deep down inside myself, I believe I can.

Skeet skeet.

26 More for the geeks... Appoggiatura: Origin: German. Meaning: A grace note performed before a note of the melody and falling on the beat.

27 Origin: French. Meaning: A part of a newspaper or magazine devoted to fiction, criticism, or light literature.

CHAPTER 3

HOW TO ACQUIRE MORE SKILLS

Before we move forward, I need to have a "real talk" moment with you.

I've never believed in the whole "you can be anything or anyone you want to be if you just put your mind to it" concept. That's fantasy thinking, and fantasy thinking isn't going to help you on your journey to millionaire status.

Everyone has different skillsets, depending on factors like life experience, work history, education, and so on. What's more, everyone has different strengths and weaknesses that make it easier or more difficult to acquire certain skills and excel in different fields. If you want to make the best use of your abilities and develop your skills in the most efficient way possible, you'll need to have some sense of your strengths and your weaknesses.

In my experience, people differ in their:

Tolerance for pain (emotional and physical)
Tolerance for risk
Fears and anxieties

Level of patience
Attention to detail
Desire or ability to socialize
Ability to focus[28]

Perhaps most importantly, people vary in their types of intelligence.

The idea of different intelligence types originated in 1983, when developmental psychologist Howard Gardner published his book "Frames of Mind: The Theory of Multiple Intelligences." For the purposes of my book, you can think of your intelligence type as a natural talent or affinity; your intelligence type makes it slightly easier for you to learn or acquire certain types of skills.

Gardner determined that there are nine different types of intelligence:

1) **SPATIAL INTELLIGENCE** is the ability to think and create in three dimensions. You can easily visualize images or constructs in your mind and then bring them to life. Artists and architects have this ability. So do pilots. Chesley "Sully" Sullenberger, the pilot of US Airways Flight 1549, called upon this type of intelligence when he decided that a water landing in the Hudson River was the only viable option to save his passengers and crew.

2) **LOGICAL-MATHEMATICAL INTELLIGENCE** is the ability to manipulate numerical data and identify, arrange, and

28 I watched a documentary in which both Warren Buffett and Bill Gates were asked to choose one word that accounts for their tremendous success. Independently, they each chose the same word: FOCUS. Once you decide to make the commitment to become a millionaire, you must focus the majority of your resources (time, money, and energy) into making that commitment a reality. If two of the richest people on the planet think focus is important, maybe we ALL need to be **teachable** enough to listen.

create connections with highly abstract and complex patterns. If keeping your checkbook balanced is an intellectual challenge for you, this probably is not your type of intelligence.

3) **MUSICAL INTELLIGENCE** involves being able to recognize pitch, rhythm, tone, etc. When you listen to music, can you hear and name the different instruments utilized to produce the song? Can you identify a song's key? Are you able to play instruments "by ear" – even ones you've never played before?

4) **BODILY-KINESTHETIC INTELLIGENCE** requires a perfect connection between the mind and the body. These people can easily translate their thoughts into actions, and they often excel at a physical activity. Michael Jordan had a high level of this intelligence when it came to playing basketball. The best mechanics and surgeons possess this type of intelligence, too.

5) **LINGUISTIC INTELLIGENCE** manifests through the ability to express yourself using spoken or written language. Do you love words? Do you get a genuine thrill out of creating connections between words? Do foreign languages come easily to you? If so, you likely possess linguistic intelligence.

6) **NATURALIST INTELLIGENCE** is the ability to identify patterns among living things. You not only enjoy being outdoors, but you feel connected to nature. You can easily distinguish one tree or flower type from another. The same thing applies to types of birds, weather patterns, rock formations, and bodies of water. This type of intelligence also applies to those who are gifted in the kitchen. The

ability to tastefully combine ingredients into an original, yet palatable, dish requires this intelligence.

7) **EXISTENTIAL INTELLIGENCE** is the ability to reflect on the human condition and the meaning of life. This group spends their time and energy attempting to understand life and death and why we are here. A quote by author Mark Twain best represents this group: "The two most important days in your life are the day you are born and the day you find out why."

8) **INTRA-PERSONAL INTELLIGENCE** is basically another way to say "self-awareness." It's understanding yourself, your motivations, and your interactions with others. If you find yourself frequently in conflict with others in multiple settings (on the job, at home, in traffic, in the supermarket, etc.), you may have low intelligence in this area.

9) **INTERPERSONAL INTELLIGENCE** manifests through the ability to understand and relate to others. Often, people with highest levels of this intelligence can suppress their own needs/desires to meet the needs/desires of others. They also tend to be good at reading people.

Your intelligence type, combined with other factors, will play a significant role in your ability to acquire and develop marketable skills. It will also, to some extent, determine *how* you develop those skills.

I've spoken to many people who believe that they just aren't wired for traditional classroom education. I strongly disagree with this. The issue is not whether you are "wired" this way or that, or whether you are in a classroom or a less formal setting. In my opinion, it's all about the subject matter – and your connection (or lack thereof) to what you are learning. In other words: If it's not something you care about, and if you don't see how it will help you in the long run, you aren't going to be especially motivated to master the material.

Now, I am not saying that everyone must have a certain amount of classroom education. But I am saying that everyone should make some sort of effort to acquire formal knowledge and/or training – as long as that formal training meets three criteria:

1) It must be interesting to you;
2) It must align with your intelligence type; and
3) It must have financial value.

Notice that I didn't say a word about getting a degree. That is intentional. When you take courses just to get a degree, you can sometimes lose the motivation needed to press forward to the end. People who lose that motivation often end up dropping out of college; they lose interest, and they fail to see how the material they're learning relates to them or their future careers.

But those people shouldn't stop learning. I know plenty of people who have decided that college or formal classroom education wasn't for them, but I don't know *anyone* who isn't interested in learning or experiencing something new. For example, you may not have the musical intelligence or motivation necessary to become a concert pianist – but if someone offered to teach you how to play your favorite song on the piano, you'd probably be game.[29]

Depending on your age, it's probably safe to assume that, by now,

29 Okay, I'll admit that learning to plink out "Get Low" on the piano has zero financial value. But it would be a fun thing to show off at parties. Even millionaires need a few dumb human tricks.

you have a set of skills that you have acquired through a combination of work experience, education, and natural aptitude. You have a platform by which you can go on to bigger and better things.

Here's an example from my own life: My first job after residency was with an emergency medicine staffing group. After one year of working with this organization, I was given the opportunity to become a shareholder. The benefits of becoming of shareholder were not solely financial, though: I now had the right and privilege to attend the company's board meetings. Although I was never a voting board member during my 10-year tenure with the company, I attended at least 95% of the meetings during that time. In the board meetings, I learned the way our business operated, the key players within our organization, and the important folks in the hospitals that we staffed. As the years went by, I became more ingrained in my group *and* in the hospital. I was learning a lot, but I also started noticing that people were interested in hearing my thoughts and opinions. These series of events led to my appointments as a medical director and a member of the compensation and medical executive committees.

Becoming a board member not only helped me advance within my chosen field, but it also helped me develop a set of secondary skills. For example, I'm an introvert by nature, so public speaking was never at the top of my priorities in life. Even today, I don't naturally gravitate to public speaking opportunities, but I can do so now – with confidence – when called upon. I also know how to conduct meetings. After a decade of sitting in on ER staff meetings, department meetings, committee meetings, medical executive meetings, and board meetings, I learned how to participate and – more importantly – run a meeting.

What I'm trying to say is that everyone starts somewhere. The skills and experience that you pursue today will lay the foundation for the skills and experience that you will attain in the future. Consider this:

Most (if not all) professional sport coaches were players in junior high, high school, and/or college.

Many film directors and producers started out as production assistants or actors.

Judges start out as lawyers.

A salesperson can become a store manager, a regional director, or vice president of sales simply by continuing to develop themselves and their skills.

The unpaid internship one summer (in any number of industries) may lead to countless lucrative opportunities in the future.

Keep in mind, though, that things don't always have to be so linear:

Steve Jobs took a calligraphy course that eventually led to the creation of fonts on the Mac.

NASA engineer Lonnie Johnson came up with the best-selling SuperSoaker water gun while he was trying to develop a heat pump that could use water in place of Freon.

The scientists who invented Viagra were trying to create a blood pressure medicine. Instead, they created a drug that increased blood flow to the penis.

Another thing to keep in mind:

Book knowledge means nothing without real-world experience.

Part of my medical training involved running what are called "mock codes." A mock code is essentially a drill; a simulation where you practice and prepare for treating a certain type of patient or specific type of illness or injury.

I'll tell you this, though: No amount of mock codes will prepare you for the real thing. You *think* you know how to treat a critically ill infant; you *think* you're ready - until you're in the ER when the paramedics rush in doing chest compressions on a five-month-old baby who is not breathing and is visibly bluish-gray. And all the while, you've got a frantic mother screaming and begging you to help.

Mock codes typically last about 10 minutes or less. In real life, you're looking at 30 minutes to an hour at the least. When you run a mock code, you focus on providing treatment and going through the motions to acquire the muscle memory.

You never practice having to tell an anxious family that their little baby has died. The real world teaches you how to hold that mother up when she wants to collapse to the floor. You see the tears, you hear the dismay, and you feel the pain.

The classroom gave me the knowledge to handle the situation, but the real world taught me how to respond.

This is true for people in every line of work, from ER physicians to teachers to professional athletes. You might think that you know sh*t, but until you're out there doing that sh*t for money and gaining actual experience, you really don't know sh*t.

Don't worry: We all start out not knowing sh*t. This is a normal and essential part of acquiring skills. If you want to be a millionaire, you *must* keep acquiring skills.

How can you learn more sh*t? Here are just a few suggestions:

- Take on new projects at work.
- Volunteer with an organization that interests you.
- Join a networking group.
- Read books.
- Watch documentaries or TED Talks.
- Take a class at your local community college.
- Watch a Khan Academy lecture.[30]
- Talk to people who have more experience than you do.

This isn't an exhaustive list, but it should be enough to get you thinking. Decide what you want to learn, and decide how you want to learn it. Remember to be teachable and open to acquiring new skills and building on your combination of intelligence type, education, and work experience. Be honest about your abilities, strengths, and weaknesses, and focus on acquiring skills that make sense for you.

Most importantly, focus on skills that will help you maximize the amount of money you can make.

I love it when I watch a TV program and an actor who has been on the show for several seasons is now directing or producing an episode (yes, I'm one of those dorks who actually watches the

30 We'll talk about side hustles later on in the book, but this is a great example: In 2008, hedge fund analyst Sal Khan created a few online tutorials to help his 12-year-old cousin with her math homework. Word spread to more of Khan's cousins, and soon they were requesting online tutorials in chemistry and other subjects. In 2009, Khan left his hedge fund job to launch Khan Academy, which offers free video tutorials on just about any STEM-related topic. Today, Khan Academy is a million-dollar-plus nonprofit organization.

credits). I like to think that they came to the realization about their extremely finite time in front of the camera and the need to develop new skills.[31] I wonder how many actors have director or producer potential but spend too much time in their trailers between takes waiting to shoot their next scene. In my opinion, they are not taking full advantage of the opportunity to build up their skills.

I also like to imagine that former athletes who are now coaches put in the time to become students of the game by watching hours and hours of game film. Development of this skill is what allowed them to transition to their new role.

You don't need a glamorous job like Hollywood actor or professional athlete in order to do this. You can do this in any industry. Most people look down on those working in the fast food industry. Not me. For those who have the right mindset, there is a significant opportunity to learn the skills necessary to run a multi-million-dollar business. The majority of workers only focus on their assigned tasks, like manning the grill or working the fryer. But that's just the grunt work. If you take a 30,000-foot-view, you could focus on finding out the answers to questions like this:

Why did the owner choose this location?
How do we obtain our supplies?
How do we hire our employees?
How do we market our location?
Which items sell well? Which ones don't?
What time of day/year is it the busiest?
What can I learn from my manager or the owner?
Can I one day manage this franchise?
Can I one day manage a region of franchises?
Can I one day own my very own franchise?

31 We'll discuss this more in Chapter 12, "You Will Be Dead Someday."

In business, a common saying is, "If you're not growing, you're dying."

Companies are always thinking of ways to increase revenue, either through the creation of new products and services or through the acquisition of new customers via increased sales or expansion into new geographies.

Think about it: Where would Apple be today if their best-selling product on the market was still the iPod? A better question to contemplate is: Where will the company be in 10 years if their bestselling product is *still* the iPhone? Businesses know that growth is essential not only for profitability, but for viability as well.

This line of thinking not only applies to businesses, but also to people. **IF YOU'RE NOT GROWING YOUR SKILLS** (financially speaking), **YOU'RE DYING** (also financially speaking).

Even though I have a medical degree and am a practicing physician, I never felt as though I could rest on my laurels. My skillset, while somewhat valuable, is by no means unique. If I don't keep growing and developing my skills, I'll become obsolete in the next 10 years. I consciously choose to grow my skills by reading at least 12 books a year, attending three to four conferences, and learning from those who are more successful than me.

What are *you* doing to grow yourself?

DON'T CONFUSE INTELLIGENCE WITH EXPERIENCE

As I have progressed through my career, I've learned the following life-changing truth:

Most people who are better than you at a certain skill aren't smarter than you.
They've simply been practicing that skill much longer than you have.

Imagine that a friend invites you over to watch "Game of Thrones" or "The Wire" or any long-running TV series with a complicated plot. You've never seen a single episode. Now imagine that you are watching, say, the fifth episode of the third season.

You and your friend are going to have very different experiences, to say the least.

*Your friend: F*ck. I can't ... this is the worst thing to happen since the Red Wedding. F*ck you, George R.R. Martin.*
You: Hold on. Who's the short guy? Who's Jon Snow? Wait, is that – are they brother and sister?! Gross.
*Your friend: Oh, sh*t! Omar just shot that guy! About time! Sweet revenge!!!*
You: Who is Omar? What's he so pissed off about? How did he get that scar? Where do you even get a gun that big?

Now let's say your friend pauses the show and gives you a quick, Cliff Notes version of the past two and a half seasons.

As you listen, do you think, "He knows *so much* about pop culture. He is so much smarter than me"? Of course not because you know this has nothing to do with intelligence. Your friend started watching the program before you did. He has more experience with the show than you do.

Writer Malcolm Gladwell popularized the concept of the "10,000-hour rule," which states that if you want to become world-class in any field, you have to spend at least 10,000 hours deliberately practicing that discipline. Many of us don't deliberately practice our skills to reach a world-class level, but when we do something repeatedly we tend to get better just through experience.

All too often, we make the mistake of confusing intelligence and experience – especially when it comes to skills-based or work-related settings. I used to attend meetings and be afraid to speak for fear of looking or sounding stupid. After some time, I started to realize that these people weren't smarter than me, but "started watching the program" months, years, or even decades earlier. Information that was new to me was already familiar to them.

In elementary school, the average third grader is more advanced than the average first grader. In sports, a rookie – even a talented rookie – is usually not the best player on the team. In residency training, the senior residents usually know more and can do more than the first-year interns.

So, the next time you encounter someone you think is more intelligent than you, please re-examine that situation from a different viewpoint. Think to yourself, "How long has this person been doing this?"

The likely answer is, longer than you have.

CHAPTER 4

WHAT IS YOUR SKILL WORTH?

I don't watch a lot of TV. My friends think I have awful taste when it comes to the programs I do enjoy watching. They're probably right. Most people have never heard of the shows I like – mostly because most of the shows I have truly liked were cancelled after just one season.

Examples include:

- "Windfall" (a group of friends win the lottery)
- "Journeyman" (guy who can travel back and forth through time)
- "The Event" (aliens living on Earth)
- "Forever" (a guy who is immortal)

No matter how much I try and defend the quality of those programs (and my rationale for watching them), it doesn't matter what I think. The market has decided.

The universe is talking back to me, and the message is loud and clear: *Paul, your TV tastes really do suck.*

It also doesn't matter that I have never watched a full episode of "The Voice," "The Big Bang Theory," "The Walking Dead," "Empire," or "This is Us," which are some of the most successful shows on TV right now. The market has spoken.

Another way of saying "the market" is "the majority."

I want to share something with you that I hope will minimize your frustration as you proceed along your millionaire journey: Your individual beliefs, morality, and ethics do not matter and cannot sway the majority.

You may believe that there is too much profanity or sex on TV. You may believe that the legalization of recreational marijuana use is bad. You might believe that Android is better than Apple; that gold is the next hot investment; that the song "Get Low" is crap; that soccer is boring; or that professional athletes make way too much money.

And you know what? If I haven't made it clear by now, let me state it again:

THE MARKET DOESN'T CARE WHAT YOU BELIEVE.

Beliefs can be dangerous because we say and do anything and everything we can to defend them, no matter if they're "wrong." This is because our beliefs are primarily ego-based and serve as our foundation. They also connect us to the world and those around us. Are you a Democrat or a Republican? Christian, Muslim, or atheist? NRA member or pro-gun control?

Our beliefs are what make us think that we (and those who think like us) "get it" and that those who don't are just a bunch of idiots.

Beliefs are very dangerous when it comes to achieving financial success. We have seen what happens to companies that hold steadfast in their belief of what the market needs or desires. Here are some examples from the last 15 or 20 years:

- Blockbuster Video[32] believed that they could ignore the rise of Netflix and continue to focus on brick-and-mortar stores, complete with late fees, limited stock, etc. By the time they made a halfhearted attempt to get in on the DVD-by-mail action, they were several years too late to the party. The company went out of business in 2011.

- In the early 2000s, Circuit City believed that it needed to compete with Best Buy to survive, so the company ditched its extremely successful appliance business and did away with its highly trained, commissions-based sales staff. As a result, they lost their profitable appliance business to DIY stores like Lowe's and Home Depot – and they continued to lose business to Best Buy until 2009, when the company declared bankruptcy.

- Research in Motion, the company responsible for the best-selling BlackBerry phone, believed in taking the "if it ain't broke, don't fix it" approach when the iPhone and other Android-based phones hit the market in the mid-2000s. Even after consumers clearly demonstrated a preference for apps or touchscreens instead of buttons, Research in Motion refused to make any significant changes. They also believed that, because they were

32 For the younger readers: Blockbuster Video was a big f*cking deal in the late 80s and early 90s. Before Netflix and Apple TV and other streaming services, if you wanted to watch a movie, you got in the car, drove to Blockbuster, and – if the movie you wanted wasn't out of stock – you stood in line for upwards of 15 to 20 minutes to rent it. And if you returned your movie late, they hit you with late fees.

the leading smartphone manufacturer, they'd stay that way... no matter what the other guys were doing.

- For around 100 years, Kodak was an industry-leading manufacturer of cameras and film in the U.S. But the company made a few critical missteps that led to its demise. The first one was in the mid-80s, when they passed on the chance to be the official camera of the Olympics. The opportunity then went to Fuji, a Japanese company that was new to the U.S. At the time, Kodak didn't think this was a big deal – the company believed that American consumers would be loyal to them, no matter what. That was a mistake, as Fuji became one of Kodak's biggest rivals. The second big misstep was refusing to give up on film while other companies went digital. Kodak believed that digital photography wasn't a big threat – and they believed that customers would always prefer film.[33]

The same thing happened in the 2008-09 financial crisis. Everyone believed the home-buying frenzy would last and that home prices would never come down. This is how bubbles happen: Everyone is believing at the same time. Beliefs are extremely powerful. History and logic are usually ineffective in changing beliefs. It usually takes an extraordinarily significant negative event to alter a belief. Lehman Brothers going bankrupt, a global stock market collapse, and the risk of another Great Depression did the trick last time... but I'm not optimistic enough to say that history won't repeat itself.

To avoid falling victim to this ever-present human flaw, please remember the following:

33 This story is even worse when you consider that Kodak basically invented digital photography!

The ratings of a show, the sales of a product, the jobs available in a city, the salaries for a position, or the price of an asset will move in whatever direction the market decides. What you believe will never, ever matter in your financial journey.

This is the reason why you have to look at all the decisions that you make as objectively as possible. It is okay to be optimistic or pessimistic at times, but you should mostly remain neutral. Neutrality allows you to remove yourself and your beliefs from the situation and evaluate things more objectively.

Okay, here comes the difficult part. I want you to use this same line of reasoning when it comes to evaluating your skills and your choice of profession.

You may think that you deserve to be paid more. Many of us may agree that teachers are grossly underpaid based on the importance of their profession. On the opposite end of the spectrum, many people cannot believe the amount of money that professional athletes and certain celebrities make.

That doesn't seem fair now, does it? Nope... because the market determines how much you will be compensated, and the market IS NOT FAIR.

For example, the market is *not* going line up outside Mrs. Anderson's 4th grade classroom to hear her talk about American history. Nobody is going to give her a multi-million dollar contract to lecture about the Constitution, and the paparazzi are unlikely to camp out in her yard to get a picture of her and her latest love interest so that they can turn around and sell it to TMZ for hundreds of thousands of dollars. Whether we believe that it's fair or not, the market has spoken - and it has decided that history teachers are not as valuable as, say, J.J. Watt or Lil Jon. So, poor Mrs. Anderson makes considerably less than they do.[34]

Now, it would be easy to say that this is because the market doesn't care about history - but I don't think that's the case. Look at the incredible success of Lin-Manuel Miranda and his Broadway smash "Hamilton." The show has been sold out for months, and really good tickets can cost up to $800 or $900. All that for a musical about the first U.S. Secretary of the Treasury!

Every action's an act of creation.

Lin-Manuel found a way to do two pretty amazing things: First of all, he took a potentially dry subject (U.S. history) and made it entertaining, interesting, and engaging. At the same time, he revolutionized the Broadway musical, blending traditional musical theater, hip-hop, and pop in a way that hadn't really been done before.

Of course, to write "Hamilton," Lin-Manuel needed to have several skills: acting, writing, music, and so on. Again, these are all skills that the market has decided are worth a lot of money. If Mrs. Anderson doesn't have those skills, it's unlikely that she will reach the same level of success. Perhaps if she is a truly amazing teacher, she might earn a raise or make a

34 If you want to see a hilarious take on the whole underpaid teachers/overpaid athletes issue, Google "Key & Peele TeachingCenter".

little more money than the first-year teacher down the hall. But nobody is going to pay $800 to hear her lecture about the Civil War or the American Revolution. If Mrs. Anderson wants to become a millionaire, she's going to have to come up with a more lucrative side hustle.[35]

As long as you have a baseline level of skill, you will be paid what those of similar skillsets are paid. Let me offer a few examples:

- If you have the skills to be an NFL starting quarterback, you are going to be paid several million dollars. Funny thing is, even if you aren't very good (i.e., if you spend most of the season sitting on the bench), you will still be paid within a range that some consider excessive.

- If you are a corporate executive who does a poor job of managing your company and loses money for shareholders, you still may still earn extremely high bonuses and receive a golden parachute upon leaving the company.

- Community hospital-based ER docs are paid in $/hr. Guess what? Even the subpar docs – the ones I wouldn't trust to take care of my family members – are still very well compensated.

Do you <u>believe</u> that you work harder on the job than someone else, produce better quality work, but are paid the same, slightly more, or significantly less? If so, it probably pisses you off, but what you <u>believe</u> doesn't matter. The market has spoken. Getting pissed off does you no good. You're just wasting unnecessary thought and energy.

35 I'll talk more about the art of the side hustle in chapter 11.2, "How I Started My Side Hustle."

There's a quote from Michelangelo that I think of any time I get pissed off about something that I believe is unfair:

Although Michelangelo said this 500+ years ago – long before people were bitching about stupid song lyrics, reality TV, overpaid athletes, or underpaid teachers – I think that his message still rings true.

To me, "criticize by creating" means, if you don't like something, stop complaining and being pissed off about it and DO SOMETHING about it. Think "Keeping Up with the Kardashians" is a stupid show? Come up with something better – AND something that the market believes is more valuable than what Kim, Kourtney, and Khloe have to offer.

Are you angry about the lack of women in STEM fields? Fed up with the lack of diversity at the Oscars? Convinced that your company is doing a sh*tty job keeping up with the competition? Do you believe your boss or supervisor is an idiot? Or your "friend" shouldn't be flashing how wonderful their life and relationships are all over their Facebook page?

It's easy to spend our time and energy worrying about what

everyone else is doing with their lives. It's also easy to throw our hands up and say, "I give up. That's how society is, and that's how it's always gonna be."

What isn't as easy is taking that worry and frustration and pissed-off energy and using it to try and change things – to *criticize* something we think is unfair or wrong by *creating* something new.

In other words:

I like to think that, if Michelangelo were alive today, this would be one of his favorite phrases. "Don't hate the player, hate the game" is our generational equivalent of "Criticize by creating."

In this modern example, "hating the player" is synonymous with criticizing something that you believe is dumb, worthless, unfair, etc. Criticizing – or "hating the player" is a waste of time. Instead, focus your energy on "hating the game": Look at the world around you, and make changes (or “creating”).

Instead of spending time hating on Kim Kardashian because she’s famous for doing nothing or criticizing your boss for mismanaging the company, do something productive and creative; contribute something that you think is valuable. Work toward changing society in some way.

Who knows? Maybe you’ll create something so popular – something that society believes is so valuable – that people will start hating on you, too.

MONEY HAS NO CONSCIENCE. PEOPLE SOMETIMES DO.

Money is indifferent to whether the application of your skills creates a positive or negative societal outcome. Life is not - and never will be - fair. The "good guy" doesn't always win, and the "bad guy" may never lose. If you're a good person but don't have the right skills, you will not make much money.

Conversely, you could be a terrible person and amass a large fortune. Drug lords, sex traffickers, and Ponzi scheme masterminds can accumulate a significant amount of wealth despite being on the wrong side of the law. Remember, it's not their fault: **The market has determined, time and time again, that there are people who want the services and/or products that these individuals are able to provide.**

Whatever your moral stance, these people have skills that the market has deemed valuable. Think about it. Could you organize and run a criminal enterprise? I know I couldn't - and I consider myself a fairly intelligent guy. I'll admit that I don't even know where to buy a small amount of cocaine, let alone the quantity required for mass distribution.

And I know nothing about the market for cocaine: Who is my competition? Based on the movies, it's probably the Colombians. Where do I find people to do the dirty work? I know that there may be some unsavory types lurking on Craigslist. How do I find corrupt cops to pay off to keep my business going? Do I just walk up to one who I perceive to be a little shady and say, "Hey, you looking to make some extra money?" And call me a wuss, but I'm not killing anyone or their innocent loved ones to protect "my territory."

There are very particular skills required to succeed in the drug underworld. The same thing goes for sex trafficking. Smuggling drugs is one thing, but smuggling people requires a different set of skills and ethics altogether.

Please let me be clear. I am not advocating nor glorifying the life of a criminal mastermind. The entertainment industry already does that for us with movies like "The Godfather" and "Goodfellas" and shows like "Breaking Bad" and Netflix's "Narcos" (based on the life of former Colombian drug lord Pablo Escobar). I am also not recommending that these are the skills you should acquire.

I am simply making the point that money flows to those with "valuable" skills.

CHAPTER 5

ARE YOU BEING APPROPRIATELY COMPENSATED FOR YOUR SKILL?

Although I'm a doctor, the market has determined that my skillset as an emergency physician is not worth as much as someone who specializes in neurosurgery, orthopedics, or cardiology. In fact, if you google "highest paid medical specialties," emergency medicine doesn't even crack the top 10.

I chose emergency medicine for a variety of personal reasons: These high-paying specialties are extremely competitive, and I may not have matched with a residency. These specialties also come with very grueling residencies/fellowships, and the lifestyle required to do well as a neurosurgeon or orthopedist would have probably sent me to an early grave.

This is why, instead of complaining about the fact that I don't make as much money as a neurosurgeon or an orthopedist, I chose to focus my energies on making damn sure that I was compensated appropriately for my work as an ER doctor.

Whether you're a neurosurgeon, a teacher, a professional athlete, or a retail salesperson, you have a certain skillset (if you need a reminder, go back to page 36 and check out what you wrote down). Regardless of what your skillset is, your journey to millionaire status must start with an objective look at what the market rate is for that skill. You may not look at people from this viewpoint, but everyone has a market rate, including you.

And remember, you need to focus on the facts – not what you believe. Hell, most people believe that they are underpaid for the work that they do. However, upon closer examination, they don't realize that the job they are being paid to do can easily be done by someone else who is equally or more qualified.

If I were a fast food worker, I'm pretty sure that I could get a job at any number of franchise brands with similar pay pretty quickly. There are more fast food jobs than people to fill them. That industry also has a lot of turnover.

However, if my skill were highly specialized and specific to an industry, then I'd need to have enough self-awareness to recognize that I may never be able to make this level of compensation ever again in my life.

No case drives this point home more clearly than what happened to former NBA player Latrell Sprewell. In 2004, Latrell turned down a three-year, $21 million contract from the Minnesota Timberwolves because he believed that amount was not enough to take care of his family. While I applaud his desire for wanting more money, Latrell (and his agent) did not think things through fully. He was near the end of his career, he didn't have the most pristine of reputations, and, most importantly, he had a highly specialized skill (playing basketball) that is only compensated extremely well in one place (the NBA).

If Microsoft, Walmart, or Exxon valued having superstar athletic talent on their roster, Latrell may have found a safe place to land. However, Latrell's skillset was so specialized that, outside of the confines of the NBA, his market value was essentially zero.

If you are going to spend the majority of your life working for someone else, it is imperative that you are well-compensated for your role. I define "well-compensated" as being in the top 10% to 25% for your position.

However, I strongly caution you not to make the Latrell Sprewell mistake and overvalue yourself.

You may believe that you deserve more money, but if you had to go out and find a new job, how easy would it be for you to get the amount of money you desire?

ARE YOUR SKILLS PORTABLE?

Before we move on, I want to make one thing very clear: You need to *make sure that your skills are portable because not all skills are*. Your skills belong to you, and the skills you develop will accompany you to future positions in other companies or industries. However, you must be aware that there may not be a place for those skills in other companies or industries.

Latrell Sprewell is a great example of this. He had one very specialized skillset: He could play basketball, which meant that he could run fast, jump high, and score baskets with a fair degree of consistency. And while this skillset served him well during his time as a professional athlete, he hasn't been able to successfully transfer those skills to another career in a different industry. Since his career-killing decision to turn down a lucrative contract, he has appeared in a commercial and a handful of podcasts.

Luckily, the vast majority of us don't have such highly specialized, niche skills.

As a doctor, my skills are diagnosing and treating patients – and while those serve me well in the ER, I could easily take those skills and combine them with my medical director/executive skills to launch a career teaching or leading quality initiatives for a hospital system. I could also freelance as a healthcare consultant.

If you're a high school teacher, your skills include the ability to learn information and explain it to others in a clear way. You are good at communicating, and you are able to manage and work with a lot of people at once. If you lose your job, you could easily take those skills and work as a private tutor. You could take those skills overseas and teach English in Dubai or Tokyo. You could leave education altogether and use your skillset to become a corporate trainer. You could write or edit textbooks.

If you are a ballet dancer, your primary skills involve one specific type of dance. But you're probably also good at working with others, you're probably quite disciplined and fit, and you've likely got a high degree of bodily-kinesthetic intelligence. You could teach ballet to kids, you could do choreography for stage or film, or you could take your existing skills and apply them to a new field: You might be a good yoga instructor or physical therapist.

Entrepreneurs typically move from project to project, and each new endeavor provides an opportunity to develop new skills and learn valuable lessons that they can apply to the next business venture. They learn how to raise money and capital; they learn how to network; they learn how to pitch their ideas to investors.

Every skill you acquire is portable. It belongs to you, and it is yours to apply in any way you see fit. The more skills you have, the more opportunities you'll have and the more adaptable you'll be.

Here are a few examples of this:

Home Depot founders Bernie Marcus and Arthur

Blank were fired from their jobs at Handy Dan Home Improvement Centers. They took their knowledge and skills and went on to found Home Depot, one of the most successful home improvement chains in the country.

With the help of his high school friend Steve Wozniak, Steve Jobs founded Apple in the late 1970s. In the mid-80s, Jobs was ousted from Apple. He took his portable skills – creativity and technical knowhow – to Hollywood, where he got into movie effects. He went on to become CEO of Pixar.

Entertainment is full of people who have taken their skills and done something new: Will Smith, LL Cool J, and Ron Howard all started out doing one thing and moved on/expanded (from rapper to TV actor to movie star; from rapper to TV star; from child star to director). It's also worth pointing out that entertainment is also full of examples of people who did NOT continue to develop their skills. These folks are struggling financially now. For example, some of the cast of "Happy Days" have experienced significant financial challenges as a result of not developing their skills – Ron Howard has not because he moved on to become a director.

Your goal should be to have a set of skills that you can apply in a wide variety of jobs in a wide variety of industries – and, ideally, they should be skills that you can apply anywhere in the world.

In my opinion, the most important reason that you need to have portable skills is so you can have more control over your life. Because some day, you might find yourself surrounded by a-holes, in an organization that doesn't value your contributions. You might find that you need to say F*CK IT and walk away.

And if that day comes, you'll need to have portable skills.

CHAPTER 5
WHERE ARE YOU?

Part 1: Get Thee to a Capitalist Country

Let's face this truth: If you are an average person – as in, you don't have any hopes of being an NFL star or a supermodel or a famous musician, and you don't come from money – you'll need the government's assistance if you want to achieve millionaire status.

When I say "assistance," I don't mean welfare or anything like that. What I mean is that, if you want to build wealth, you'll need to live in a nation whose laws support the creation of individual wealth. In other words: You need to live in a capitalist country.

Here is a list of capitalist countries[36] ranked by GDP:

1) United States
2) Japan
3) Germany
4) United Kingdom
5) France
6) Brazil
7) Italy
8) Canada

If you don't live in a capitalist country, you need to move to one, ASAP.

I don't know your situation, of course, but I understand that picking up and moving to a new country is a big deal. It may be one of the most difficult parts of your journey to millionaire status. You might feel scared or apprehensive, especially if you have a family to provide for, or if you'll have to learn a new language,

36 This list is certainly not meant to be exhaustive. There are many other capitalist countries out there to choose from – but these are the leaders in terms of GDP.

or if you don't know anyone who is already living in your chosen country. But if you're living in a third-world country or a country where there's no real way for you to move up in the world socially or financially[37] (think: Cuba, Venezuela, or even India) you really don't have a choice.

So, if you're reading this book and you are living in a country that actively impedes your journey to millionaire status, your first step is to do some research on different capitalist countries.

Pick a country where the laws, citizens, language, and/or culture will not bar your path to wealth. Any of the countries listed above may work. I'm probably biased when I say this, but in my opinion, the US is a good choice.

If you were born in a capitalist country, please thank your parents. And give yourself a big pat on the back: By simply being born in the right place, you've saved yourself a lot of work.

If you immigrated to a capitalist country, congratulations – but you still have a lot of work ahead of you.

Ready? Let's move on.

Part 2: I'm Here. Yay, Capitalism. Now What?

Simply moving to a capitalist country, or being born in one, won't make you a millionaire. It's a huge step in the right direction – but it's just a starting point.

---

37 I am not saying that the United States – or any other capitalist country – offers a truly equal playing field. In any country, you will encounter challenges. Your experience may be different depending on how your chosen country views your race, gender, sexual orientation, religion, or education level. But at least you have an opportunity to get onto the field.

The next step is figuring out what part of your chosen capitalist country is the best fit for you.

Because here's the thing: Even if you live in a capitalist country, you will not become a millionaire if you are living in a city, state, or province where your skills are not in demand.

Let's say your dream is to become an actor. Your skills include things like conveying emotions in a believable way, memorizing lines, performing in front of people, and maybe even singing and dancing. And let's say you live in South Dakota, where the economy is based almost entirely on the service industry, farming, and – because South Dakota is home to Deadwood, Mount Rushmore, and the annual Sturgis Motorcycle rally – tourism. As an actor in South Dakota, you might be able to get a gig doing your best Al Swearengen[38] impression at a wild-west-themed tourist trap. You could probably teach high school drama or participate in community theater. More than likely, though, you'll end up working in retail because that's what is in demand in South Dakota. If you want a real shot at stardom, you'd be better off moving to New York or Los Angeles, where there are more opportunities for people with your skillset.

Or maybe your goal is to work in the oil and gas industry. Maybe you're a pipeline service technician or a geologist. You'd be much, much better off in a state like Colorado, Louisiana, Oklahoma, North Dakota, Texas, or Utah. Your chances of having a successful career would be greatly diminished if you were living in, say, Rhode Island or Massachusetts.

And, hell, no matter *what* kind of skills you have, you'll be better

38 If you've seen HBO's short-lived series "Deadwood" you know exactly who this guy is. For those of you who spent your time doing more productive things: Al Swearengen was an "entertainment entrepreneur" (read: pimp) who ran The Gem, a successful saloon/brothel in late 1800s Deadwood, South Dakota.

off in a state, city, or province that has a high employment rate and a strong economy.

Not sure if you're living in the right place? Ask yourself the following questions:

> *Where do you live, exactly? What state, city, province, or municipality?*
>
> *Is your state, city, province, or municipality thriving? Are people moving there, or is everyone leaving due to lack of jobs?*
>
> *Are property values rising or falling?*
>
> *Are the local schools good?*
>
> *Is the cost of living reasonable?*
>
> *Does the tax structure prevent you from keeping more of what you earn?*
>
> *What are the major industries where you live?*
>
> *Are your skills in demand?*

These are the questions that eventually led me to relocate to Houston, Texas, from my native New York City. I didn't move to Houston because I had family there or knew anyone. It was mostly an economic decision. And it was partially because I never wanted to shovel snow again in my life.

After four years of college and four years of medical school, I had amassed over $160,000 in debt (which seems relatively cheap based on the cost of education today). I still remember sitting in a medical school financial aid meeting and being told about the definite possibility that I would still be paying down my student loans when my kids would be of age to attend medical school.

That was one of those "Oh, *hell* no" moments for me. It motivated me to find a position in a place that would allow me to make as much money as possible to rid myself of this burdensome debt.

ER doctors in New York City earn 30% to 50% less than ER doctors in Texas. New York also has a much higher cost of living, and residents have to pay state and city income taxes. In Texas, the cost of living is low and there is no state income tax. Unemployment is low, the economy is strong.

You need to live in an area that is flourishing because, as the saying goes, "a rising tide raises all ships." If your city is doing well, the people around you are probably doing well – and that increases the likelihood that you will also do well. How do you know which areas are flourishing? Do a quick a web search for "Fastest Growing Cities" or "Best Cities for ______ Profession."

If your city isn't on those lists AND you are not doing well financially, guess what?

YOU MUST MOVE.

If you're feeling apprehensive about relocating, I'd simply ask you to take a moment to put things in perspective: How much of a risk are you really taking? Think about the explorers who set sail from Europe in search of unknown "new worlds" to claim. Think about the first astronauts and the race to become the first person on the moon. Think about the thousands of refugees who flee war-torn countries with little more than the clothes on their backs. When you think about it like that, your move from one relatively safe state or province to another suddenly doesn't seem like such a big deal.

Some people are so reluctant to leave their hometowns that they miss out on more lucrative opportunities elsewhere. Maybe it's a combination of being comfortable and complacent; or maybe it's a strong attachment to family or friends. Unfortunately, this attachment may prevent these people from becoming millionaires.

What's more, that fear of losing touch isn't really a thing we have to worry about today: We have email and Skype to help us keep in touch with the folks back at home. Most cell phone plans have unlimited long distance. Social media keeps us connected to people we haven't seen since high school.

My philosophy has always been that if someone from India, China, Iran, Cuba, Nigeria, or the Philippines can make the journey to America, I sure as hell can move across the country if the right opportunity presents itself. Also, moving will naturally force you to develop another very important skill: being adaptable.

Part 3: When Are You?

Don't worry. I'm not getting metaphysical on you.

But I thought that I'd close this chapter with a brief discussion about how much your life is shaped by what point on the Earth's 4.5-billion-year timeline you happen to be living on. Things may not be perfect, but people living right now have a lot of advantages over previous generations.

It's like the famous quote from Warren Buffett:

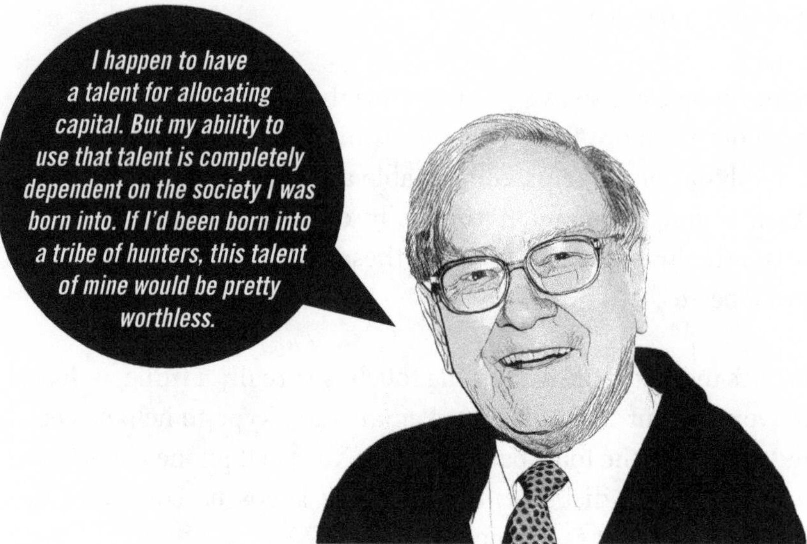

Buffett's example, while amusing, also provides insight into how he sees the world. I'm also thankful to have not been born during the hunter/gatherer age. As a black guy, though, I feel especially blessed that I wasn't born any time before 1960.

Although our world is far from perfect, I feel extremely lucky to be alive now. We live in a time and in an environment that allows those from different backgrounds, ethnicities, cultures, and varying degrees of education/social connections to become financially successful.

CHAPTER 6

ARE YOU A PRODUCER?

What value do your skills bring to those around you?
The more lives you can touch, the wealthier you will become.

Here's a quick breakdown of *just some* of the hours I've wasted watching television shows:

- "Lost": 6 seasons/121 episodes ~100 hours
- "24": 3 seasons[39]/72 episodes ~60 hours
- "Heroes": 4 seasons/83 episodes ~69 hours

At first blush, these numbers don't look too bad... but this isn't the only TV/film consumption of which I'm guilty. I also have a bad habit of re-watching TV shows and movies I've seen before. I can't tell you how many times I've seen the following movies in their entirety:

- "Armageddon"
- "Back To The Future" (including sequels)
- "Braveheart"
- "Die Hard"

39 I believe "24" had 8 seasons, but I bowed out after Season 3.

- "Die Hard 2"
- "Grease"
- "Forrest Gump"
- "A Few Good Men"
- "The Green Mile"
- "Goodfellas"
- "The Karate Kid" (the 1984 original)
- "The Karate Kid Part II"
- "The Matrix" (including sequels)
- "Remember The Titans"
- "Rocky III"
- "Rocky IV"
- "The Shawshank Redemption"
- "Star Wars" (including prequels *and* sequels)
- "Superman"
- "Superman II"
- "Terminator 2: Judgement Day"
- "Titanic"[40]
- "Iron Man" (including sequels)
- "The Avengers"
- "Frozen"[41]

For the sake of example, let's say that I've seen each of these movies at least four times (I'm being easy on myself). If you assume that each movie is at least two hours long, then I've spent more than 400 hours watching these movies. Again, this is a gross underestimation of my overall TV/movie visual consumption. Thank God I'm not a fan of the "Lord of the Rings" or "Hobbit" trilogies... each of those films is well over three hours long!

Over the past several years, multiple people have told me that I need to watch the TV series "Breaking Bad." Without fail, each

40 I have *no* idea why I like this movie so much.

41 I have daughters who share my tendency to re-watch movies they've seen before.

and every person making the recommendation has said, with the greatest of enthusiasm, that it is The Best TV Show Ever Made.

Despite all of these glowing recommendations, I haven't seen a single episode of "Breaking Bad." This is not because I don't want to watch "Breaking Bad," and it's not because I don't think I'd like it. Exactly the opposite: I'm sure I'd enjoy it immensely.

The reason I haven't watched "Breaking Bad" is because I feel that I have already spent too much time consuming television and movies. And I know that if I want to maintain and grow my millionaire status, I have to spend more time being a producer and less time being a consumer. Of course, if I were, say, a television writer or a film student instead of an entrepreneurial ER physician, watching "Breaking Bad" might not be a time-waster. In fact, watching TV or movies might help me build essential skills like storytelling, pacing, or writing interesting characters and realistic dialogue.

From childhood, we are trained to be consumers; we learn that acquiring material possessions and indulging in entertainment like movies, TV, and music makes us feel good. Initially, we want relatively inexpensive things: a trip to our favorite fast food restaurant, a new toy, an afternoon at the movies, etc. As we get older, though, our desires begin to change. We want bigger and better and more expensive things: cars, clothes, handbags, vacations, homes, etc. We borrow money to help feed our appetite for consumption, and then we have to deal with consequences of debt. We eat too much food, and then have to deal with the problems associated with gaining too much weight. We binge-watch our favorite TV programs on Netflix, and then avoid spending that time taking care of more important aspects of our life, such as exercise and fitness.

Why do we do this? In my opinion, I think we are hard-wired to do what comes easy. Consuming comes easy. It requires little effort. It makes us feel good. You just need money (whether that money is yours, your parents', the bank's, the credit card company's, etc.), and whatever you want can be yours.

When you choose to consume something – whether that something is a Happy Meal, a Gucci bag, a six-bedroom McMansion, or the first season of "Breaking Bad" – you are spending money and potentially making someone else rich.

But what happens if you choose to *produce* something instead? Depending on what you produce, you are creating the opportunity to earn money and perhaps even make yourself rich.

If you have a job, you already are a producer, to some extent. Someone is willing to pay you for your time because it is assumed that your work product will result in increased revenue (read: more money) for your company. The more valuable the work you produce, the more money you are likely to earn.

If you want to become wealthy, you will have to focus most of your time, money, thoughts, and energy on producing rather than consuming.

Trust me, I get it: It's much, much easier to consume. We buy more clothes, eat more food, drink more alcohol, and watch more TV because no work and/or discipline is involved. Everyone is guilty of this, including me (minus the alcohol; I'm not much of a drinker). My weakness happens to be movies and TV, which I'll happily binge-watch instead of doing any number of more productive things.

If I'm being completely honest, I've also wasted valuable time playing video games. I can't tell you how many hours I spent playing the latest iteration of "Madden," learning a team's offensive and defensive schemes so I could destroy my online competitors. When I took my team through a simulated championship football season, I felt as though I won the Super Bowl. Same goes for the fighting game genre: Mastering fatalities in "Mortal Kombat" used to be a priority for me. If you put a controller in my hand right now, I could probably *still* execute Sub-Zero's "spine rip" without even thinking about it.[42]

I'm a pretty big Stephen Covey[43] fan, and I subscribe to his idea that everything we do in life can be divided into four quadrants:

QUADRANT 1

This quadrant is made up of actions that are very important and very urgent; they must be taken care of immediately because they affect your immediate quality of life, well-being, etc.

Examples of this might include:

- *You've just been in a car crash and you need to exchange insurance information with the other driver, seek medical attention, get your car towed to the shop, etc.*
- *Your house is on fire, and you need to get yourself, your family, and your pets outside to safety.*

QUADRANT 2

These actions are important but not quite urgent. They will affect your life and future, but they aren't life-threatening and don't have to be taken care of immediately.

Examples of this include things like:

- *Learning a new skill.*
- *Taking on new responsibilities at work.*
- *Exercising.*
- *Writing a book (for me, this book is an example of a "Quadrant 2" action. I believe it will have a positive effect on my future, but it is not an emergency).*

---

42 ➔ + ➘+ ➔ + A

43 If you haven't done so already, I suggest you read Covey's book, "The Seven Habits of Highly Effective People." Or, even better: Go for the audiobook version instead. I thought it was a difficult read (and I like to read). It offers valuable advice that will help you on your journey to millionaire status.

QUADRANT 3	QUADRANT 4
Here's where you'll find all of the actions that are urgent, but not especially important. Things that fall into this quadrant include: • *Some meetings.* • *Some phone calls.* • *Some Emails.*	This is the bottom of the barrel, priority-wise. Nothing in this category is urgent OR important; none of these actions will help you improve your life, health, or well-being. Think of this as the "time-suck" quadrant that includes: • *Binge-watching "Breaking Bad" or "The Matrix" for the 500th time.* • *Putzing around on Facebook.* • *Playing "Call of Duty," "Madden," "Halo," "World of Warcraft," etc.*

If you want to have a different life than the average person, you'll need to spend more time on Quadrant 2 activities that will help you become more of a producer and less of a consumer.

Of course, that means you'll need to spend considerably less time on the time-sucking Quadrant 4 activities. This is something to think about the next time you decide to settle down with your favorite movie/TV show/video game/social media site: *What would my life look like or what new skills could I possess if I focused that time on producing instead of consuming?*

Even better: Can you come up with your own idea for a Quadrant 4 activity? Can you create the next Angry Birds, Halo, or Instagram? Can you write the next "Breaking Bad"? If you can create the next fun distraction, you may very well become a millionaire. These activities are not a waste of time if you're on the producing side instead of the consuming side.

I'm not proud of this, but I'll admit that I've spent my fair share of time trying to get all three stars on a level in Angry Birds. I've also been known to play Words With Friends semi-obsessively. I wonder what opportunities I may have missed or which dreams were deferred because I spent too much time engaging in Quadrant 4 activities.

Are you, like me, guilty of wasting precious time?

Becoming a producer doesn't mean you have to be a super smart. You just need to be disciplined and focused with your time. You need to be ready to put Netflix on hold for a month.

A FINAL NOTE ON POP CULTURE

You might get a sense, based on this chapter, that I think TV, movies, and video games are completely worthless – this is not true at all. There's something to be said for being able to engage in pop-culture-related "water cooler talk" from time to time.

Plus, if you're the only person in your office who has never heard of "Game of Thrones" or "Mortal Kombat," you'll look like a weirdo. If you're a millionaire, it won't matter. But you'll still look like a weirdo.

My advice? Just remember that every hour you spend consuming is an hour you're *not producing*. Be selective about the entertainment you consume, and consume it in moderation.

CHAPTER 7

HOW TO THINK LIKE A PRODUCER

To become wealthy as a producer, you need to be passionate and purposeful about doing one or both of these things:

1) Creating
2) Solving "problems"

Keep in mind, I am using the word "problems" extremely liberally. Having no money in the bank to pay the rent or mortgage is a problem. Your kid getting diagnosed with cancer is a problem. If you can come up with the solution to widespread poverty or the cure for cancer, you can put this book down right now and start counting your money.

But most people don't get rich solving life-or-death, capital-P "Problems." The truth is that most people who become millionaires do so by solving what people often call "first-world" problems, like having to carry around several physical CDs in order to listen to your music library, having to return movies to the local video store (or pay late fees when you don't return them), or having to paint your own nails.

You don't even have to be especially creative or have a highly-specialized skill to solve one of these "problems." The world, and America in particular, is a place where anything is possible.

As we discussed in Chapter 4, **the market determines the value of your creation.**

People will always have the need for (and the market will always value) the following:

- Clothing
- Convenience
- Education
- Entertainment
- Exercise
- Food and Beverage
- Healthcare
- Inspiration
- Investment
- Personal Care
- Pets
- Safety
- Sex
- Shelter
- Technology
- Travel/Transportation

Let me break down each category so I can get your creative juices flowing. I will present just a few examples of people who have solved a first-world problem in a way that the market has determined to be valuable.

CLOTHING

Do you have any ideas how to make clothing better?

Football player Kevin Plank was tired of being sweaty after practice. He worked on developing a moisture-wicking fabric to solve the problem. Today, Under Armour is one of the largest athletic apparel suppliers in the world.

Florida sales rep Sara Blakely had a problem with the way her undergarments fit. She experimented with different options and eventually developed Spanx.

University of Maine freshman Gary Clegg would wrap up in a sleeping bag to stay warm in his dorm room – but he found that it was difficult to do things like reach his TV remote while he was bundled up. He cut a hole in his sleeping bag, and his mother sewed a sleeve onto it. They added another sleeve, and the sleeved blanket -- or "Slanket" (the predecessor to the Snuggie)-- was born.

CONVENIENCE

What inconvenient things do we have to do every day? Hailing a taxi used to be a pain in the butt. We used to have to wonder when the cab would arrive, if we had enough cash to pay for the fare, and how much we should tip. Companies such as Uber and Lyft have revolutionized the experience for the consumer, making use of smartphone technology to make it easy to track your ride, pay, and even review your drivers.

Think of just about any product marketed on late-night infomercials. If you're looking for a faster and easier way to cook, do your laundry, groom your dog, wax your car, or edge your lawn, you can find a product that will do the job for a small one-time payment or a few (3) low monthly payments.

EDUCATION

Most parents will spend whatever is necessary to make sure their kids have the brightest future possible or the highest test scores.

Can you come up with the next Kumon, Sylvan Learning Center, or Kaplan Test Prep? Can you create a free online educational platform like Khan Academy?

Adults will spend money, too, if you can help them pick up a new skill quickly and easily. Can you come up with the next Rosetta Stone or experiential learning course?

ENTERTAINMENT

This is an area where the landscape is completely wide open. You never know what will capture the attention and imagination of the market.

Who would have thought that, for a period of time, "Charlie Bit My Finger" would be the most-watched YouTube video on the planet? Could anyone have predicted that one of the most popular music videos in the world would be "Gangnam Style" by South Korean musician Psy?

Can you come up with television more compelling than "Keeping up with the Kardashians"? Or erotic fiction that sells more copies than "50 Shades of Grey"?

GAMES

Can you come up with the next Pokémon Go? The enthusiasm has waned a bit since it first came out, but for a while, people were so busy hunting down Charizard, Mr. Mime, or the ultra-elusive Ditto that they were wandering into traffic and falling off cliffs!

And don't forget about other kinds of games. Like game shows. At nearly 60 years old, Vanna White is still dressing up in sparkly evening gowns and flipping letters on Wheel of Fortune. I guess, if you want to get really technical about it, she doesn't really "flip" them anymore since the switch to touchscreen... but talk about finding your niche!

EXERCISE

Everyone needs exercise, but most of us don't particularly enjoy working out, and we tend to have trouble sticking with a workout routine.

People have been trying to solve this problem for decades. Before we had CrossFit, Insanity, and P90x, we had aerobics, step aerobics, and water aerobics. We had pilates, yoga, and spinning. We had Jack LaLane, Jane Fonda, Richard Simmons, and Billy Blanks. This is also why we have infomercials for the Thighmaster, the Ab Roller, Tae-Bo, and Hip-Hop Abs.

Do you have an idea that will have an impact on the industry?

FOOD AND BEVERAGE

Based on the global challenge with obesity in the developed nations, it's pretty obvious that enjoying good food and drink is at the top of everyone's priorities.

Today, fast food restaurants like McDonalds and Burger King are losing market share to a new breed of "fast-casual" restaurants that are perceived as being healthier, higher-quality, etc. There are entire stores that sell protein bars and drink mixes to help you bulk up; there are any number of books and membership-based services that will help you slim down.

Is there a new food or drink concept you have been thinking about? What concepts can you add to this market? It's an extremely crowded space and super-competitive, but you can still succeed.

HEALTHCARE

Although our lifestyle choices may say otherwise, most people want to be healthy. The problem is, the majority don't want to have to work too hard to maintain their health.

Is there something that you can create that makes people healthier and requires little effort on their part? This is the secret of the pharmaceutical industry. There is a pill on the market for just about any condition you can think of, from erectile dysfunction to hair loss.

And don't forget the multi-billion-dollar (unregulated) vitamin and supplement industry. This is another example that reflects our desire for shortcuts to better health.

INSPIRATION

Do you have the charisma and knowledge to inspire others to improve themselves or their lives?

This is how individuals such as Oprah Winfrey, Tony Robbins, and Joel Osteen have found tremendous financial success. However, each of them uses a different approach and different content to provide that inspiration.

I would include teachers, coaches, therapists, and marketing specialists as those who have the opportunity to inspire. Is there something you can create to inspire others?

INVESTMENT

Do you have the skill to grow other people's money?

This category is not for the faint of heart. But if you have the talent to make a profit, if you identify investment trends before they develop, or if you can see opportunities where others only see risk, you might have what it takes to help people invest and grow their money.

As a guy who has both made and lost a bunch of money throughout his life, here's what I have learned about being a successful investor:

1) Never invest in a startup (unless you are personally involved). Many mistakes are made as the managers are using your money to figure out what they don't know. Most leaders of startups are too overconfident, in my experience.
2) Never invest in anything you don't understand. Pretty straightforward.
3) Never invest based solely on someone's previous or current success. Most investment success has more to do with timing and market conditions than the innate ability of the leader and/or company.

PERSONAL CARE

Everyone wants to look, feel, or smell better. Is there something you or your friends wish existed that would make taking care of yourself a bit easier?

One of my colleagues told me that when she was younger, she and her sister used to take turns straightening each other's naturally curly hair with a clothes iron. She would position her head so that her hair would rest on the ironing board, and her sister would press it. I didn't know much, if anything, about hair care (and still don't), but after hearing this, I quickly realized why Farouk Shami, founder of CHI Hair Care, became a billionaire: He developed an entire line of products to help people make their hair as straight, curly, dark, light, or big as they want it.

Another good example in this area is Proactiv, a line of skincare products developed by dermatologists Katie Rodan and Kathy Fields. They developed (and eventually sold) an over-the-counter, multi-step acne treatment that has become a multi-million-dollar-per-year seller.

PETS

People love their pets and will do or spend anything on them, no different than children. Can you drum up something that makes pets live longer, healthier, or happier lives?

Twenty years ago, who would have thought that people would pay for their dogs to go to day care? By humanizing your pet, you may find hidden opportunities. Another way of saying this is, what services or products exist for people but have not yet been developed for pets?

SAFETY

An unfortunate reality is that the world has always been a dangerous place. Not only do we have to worry about another human being causing us harm, but we also must be on the lookout for animals and nature. What ideas do you have to make and keep people safe?

When I was a kid growing up in New York City, it seemed as though everyone had The Club. We put this device through the steering wheel to prevent anyone from stealing our car. Every year, there seems to be a natural disaster somewhere; do you have any creative solutions to save lives or possessions? Everyone wants their kids to be safe (both in the real world and online). What ideas do you have to protect kids?

SEX

Based on the growing global population, I assume most people are still having sex. Is there anything you can produce that can make sex more interesting or satisfying?

SHELTER

Can you develop, build, or provide housing for individuals, families, or businesses? Can you start your own architecture firm, construction company, or invest in multi-family units?

Can you create the next Trulia, AirBnB, or VRBO?

SPORTS

Are you passionate about sports? You may no longer be able to run or jump like you used to, but you don't have to. Think about using your brain instead of your body. Ten years ago, no one had heard of Tough Mudder, the 10-12-mile military-style obstacle course endurance event. The company was founded in 2010 and, by 2013, was worth over $70 million. By 2015, over 2 million people had participated in a Tough Mudder event. I think running 10-12 miles in and of itself is challenging. Who would have thought that millions of people would pay good money to climb walls, crawl through mud, and get electrocuted?

When you think about sports, think beyond the four major ones[44] - that's too conventional. Think about the consumer market. If you already have an "in" to the Big 4, though, it's probably best to figure out ways capitalize on the billions of dollars surrounding you.

Hell, you can even make pretty good money *talking* about sports. Ever heard the phrase, "Let's get ready to rumble"? Sports announcer Michael Buffer has made hundreds of millions by

44 NFL (football), NBA (basketball), MLB (baseball), and NHL (hockey).

trademarking the phrase – which means he gets paid every time it's used. Only in America...

TECHNOLOGY

This is another area that is pretty wide open, similar to entertainment. And remember when I say "technology," I'm not talking about inventing the Internet or the iPhone – I'm talking about anything that helps solve an everyday first-world problem.

You don't have to be a super-genius or have special training to come up with a great idea. Here are just a few examples of technologies that make an everyday task easier or more convenient:

- Those plastic dental floss things you can buy at the drugstore. They make it faster and easier to floss your teeth.
- If you watch late-night TV, you've seen the infomercial for "My Pillow." Some dude in Minnesota thought his pillow was uncomfortable, so he invented his own and started a multi-million dollar business enterprise.
- The George Foreman Grill was an immensely popular cooking device in the mid '90s to early 2000s. Cooking your meat on both sides at a slight downward angle to drain away unhealthy fat made the grill a smash hit with consumers.
- The mop is another technological device that's changed a lot since I was a kid. I remember my mother having to wear those yellow rubber gloves so she could wring out the mop by hand or use the attached lever located towards the bottom of the mop that you would bend backwards to squeeze the sponge. Fast forward to present day... thanks to people with ergonomically creative minds, we no longer have to bend over (or wear those nasty rubber gloves) when mopping the floor. The Miracle Mop is the brand

name we all probably know the best.[45]

- Dusting is another example. How did we ever get on before Swiffer came along?
- Duck hunters everywhere can thank Phil Robertson, star of reality TV show "Duck Dynasty," for creating The Duck Commander call.

Really, the sky's the limit here: Can you think of a creative solution to a common problem?

TRAVEL/TRANSPORTATION

Is there a better way for us to get from Point A to B?

Some years ago, the standup scooter, Segway, hit the market. While it wasn't the game-changer it was predicted to be, it still made its creator a millionaire. You can buy cars that run on electricity. The Hyperloop is being developed. Do you have a solution for rush hour?

What if none of these strikes a chord with you? Don't be afraid to aggressively brainstorm. All it will cost you is some time and energy. Also, don't set yourself up for defeat before you start. You may think that someone else already has a head start or took your one and only idea. Well, work harder than that someone else to get your offering out ahead in the market. Everyone has ideas, but not everyone can execute.

The more you are able to produce items or services of value, the more financially valuable you can become.

45 The 2015 Jennifer Lawrence movie "Joy" is about Joy Mangano, the woman who invented this mop. Yes, I also wasted time watching this one.

CHAPTER 8

KNOW YOUR POSITION

At a young age, you quickly learn that you are not the boss. The basic structure of most families is:

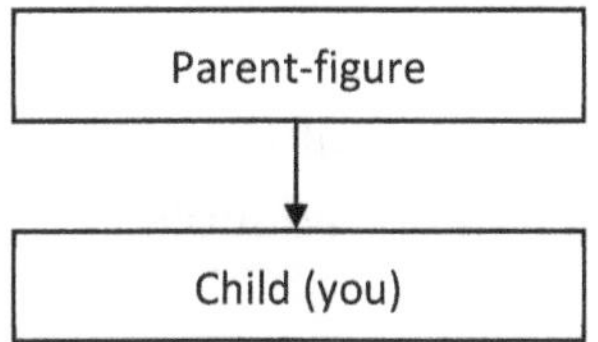

If you grew up in a "traditional" two-parent home,[46] your family structure probably looked like this:

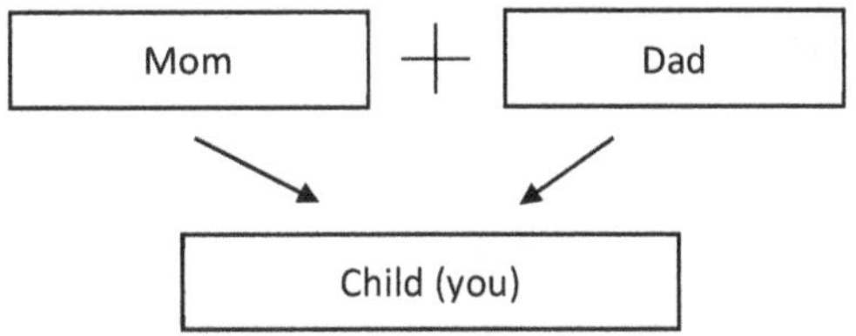

46 Of course, the definition of "traditional" is changing with the times – you might come from a family headed by two moms or two dads; or you might come from a family with step-parents and step-siblings. Or maybe you were raised by your grandparents or your aunt and uncle. Ultimately, though, there was some sort of hierarchy in place where the adult parent-figures were in charge, and you (and your siblings and step-siblings) had to listen, obey, and follow orders.

In this scenario, you had *two* bosses to listen to and obey.

Now, let's say you also had siblings, and there was a five-year age difference between you and your older siblings. Your family structure – and your position within that structure – just became a lot more complicated.

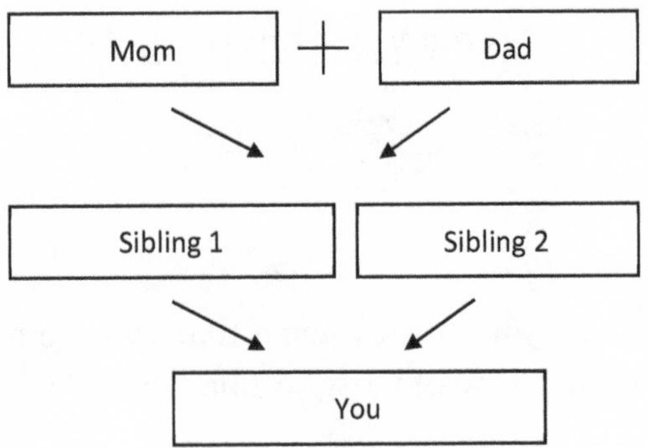

In this example, you can see that the number of people who can potentially boss you around has doubled.

If I added grandparents, aunts, and uncles, you could imagine how much farther down the power structure you could drop. However, thanks to Father Time, you eventually grow from a child to an adult and can one day sit at the top of your own family structure if you so choose.

Your work life is no different. Your position (or title[47]) within the structure of your company or your organization determines how you are treated, who gets to boss you around, what you get to do,

47 I am greatly conflicted when it comes to titles. Many people use their title and superior position to take advantage of other people and/or situations. This may be happening in your company, but don't feel as though this experience is unique to you. People in power have a tendency to abuse it. It's human nature. Power can be intoxicating. That's why teachers sometimes prey on students, parents abuse their children, or patriarchal husbands believe they have the right to treat their wives like sh*t.

who you get to interact with, *and how much money you make.*

In most cases, when you are just starting out in your chosen career, you begin at the very bottom. You're a "grunt" – everyone can boss you around, your work might not be especially challenging, and it's likely that nobody views you as a decision-maker worth listening to.

Most large companies are set up something like this:

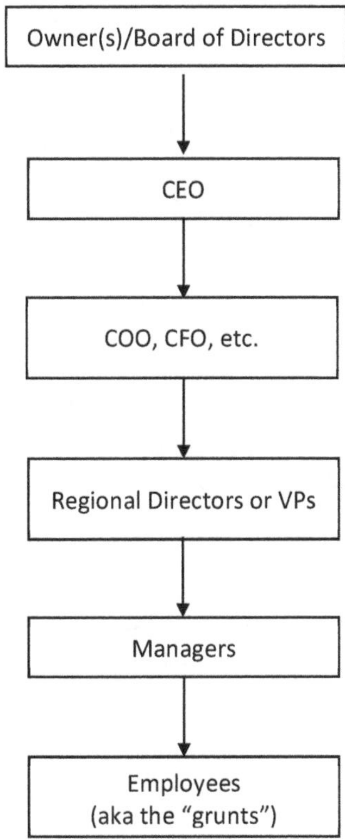

This organizational chart can apply to nearly any job with any company. At Starbucks, for example, the baristas are the "grunts" doing all the heavy lifting. From there, you have a store manager who oversees all of the baristas, and then you have a regional manager who is in charge of overseeing several stores within his or her region. Then you've got regional VPs, and so on, all the way up to the CEO.

Keep in mind that you can find grunts in ANY field or industry; the term doesn't denote a specific level of education or prestige. Grunts are simply the lowest people on the corporate/organizational totem pole; they have the least authority and usually have the least experience.[48] The grunts are typically the last to know about - but, perversely, the first to be affected by - things like pay cuts and layoffs.

A first-year high school math teacher is a grunt. He or she will have very little autonomy. Nobody will view him or her as an authority, and he or she will be bossed around by just about everyone else, from the head of the mathematics department to the assistant principal to the school district superintendent.

In the community emergency medicine world,[49] the ER doctor is the grunt; he or she has to answer to - and take direction from - the medical director, the regional medical director, hospital administration, and so on. During my first few years working in the ER, I definitely considered myself a grunt. Sure, I was a doctor. I made a good salary and enjoyed a certain degree of prestige attached to the title - but I was at the very bottom of my emergency medicine group's structure, which looked like this:

48 This is not always the case. I know people who have been operating at the "grunt" level for years - happily. They just don't have the desire to move on or grow their skills. When I was a new ER doc - a "grunt" - I was working side-by-side with docs who had been in the ER for 10+ years. They were much more experienced than I was.

49 This is entirely different from the academic medicine world (otherwise known as a teaching hospital). In that world, the interns and residents are the grunts. They do all of the heavy lifting while the attending doctors concentrate on teaching, research, and publishing.

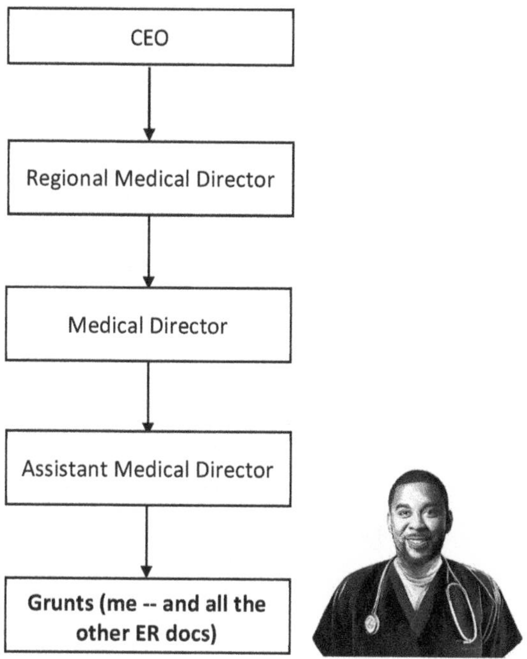

I understood my position, and I knew that, if I wanted to move up in the organization and make more money, I'd have to actively develop my skills; I'd have to find ways to interact with people higher up than I was; I'd have to seek out new responsibilities.

This meant that, in addition to performing my duties as an ER grunt, I began attending hospital committee meetings, I worked last-minute uncovered shifts, and I basically did whatever was asked of me. After a couple of years, my position changed; I moved up within my emergency medicine staffing group's structure, which now looked like this:

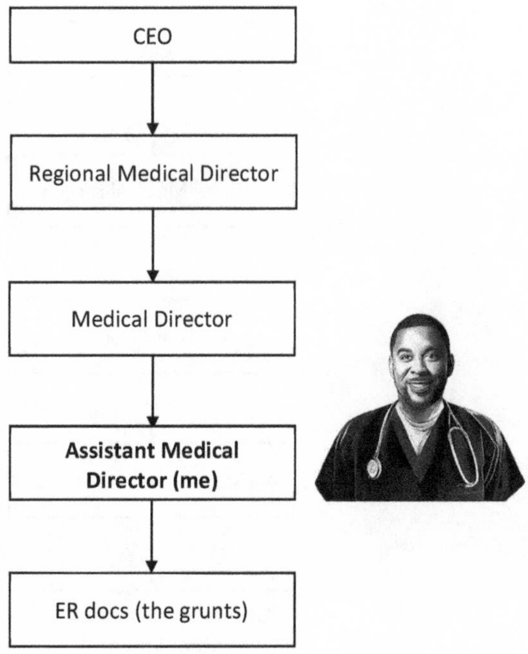

I was no longer at the very bottom; I was now partially responsible for helping manage the grunts. I was now working directly with higher-ups, and people were interested in what I had to say.

But I didn't stop there. In my new position, I continued to actively develop my skills, interact with people higher up than I was, and seek out new responsibilities. Instead of simply attending meetings, I was now helping run them. I had the opportunity to attend meetings between my medical director and the hospital CEO. If my medical director wasn't able to attend a meeting, I was seen as the de facto leader of the ER.

It turns out that having not-so-infrequent meetings with the hospital CEO during those two years allowed me to make a favorable impression on him. When he got promoted to a larger hospital, he contacted me about joining him as the medical director in the ER.

My position within my organization's structure changed again:

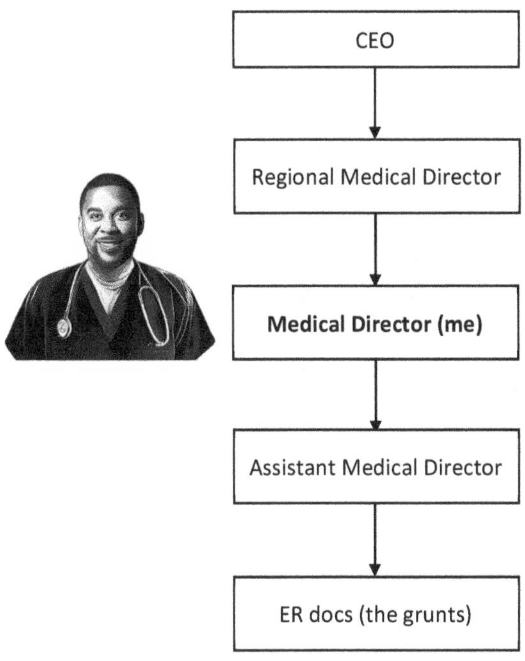

These diagrams oversimplify my progression, but you can see the point I'm trying to make. I recognized my position, I took active steps to change that position and move up within my organization, and each time I moved up, I got a new title - and a raise. This helped me move closer to millionaire status.

But that's enough about my career for the moment. Let's talk about you and your career.

Use the blank diagram to map out your company's structure - and your position within that structure:

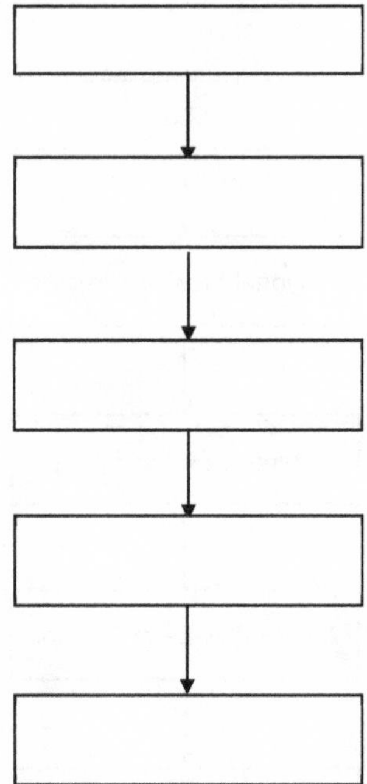

What do you do? Are you a "grunt"? Are you in the chief executive suite (C-suite)? Are you somewhere in between?

What is your title? What is the title of the person directly above you? What about the title of the person directly above them?

Do you know what steps you need to take to start moving up the ladder? Do you know what kinds of skills you need to acquire and responsibilities you need to take on in order to move up? Do you know what kind of salary increase you can expect if you continue to move up?

Of course, identifying your position is just the starting point for building wealth. Unless you are already in the C-suite (or your organization's equivalent of the C-suite), you likely aren't going to become a millionaire by staying where you are for the next five to 10 years.

This is especially true if you are one of the grunts. You spend most of your time and have most of your discussions with your fellow grunts. This is only good for a finite period of time – and if you stay too long with this group, your financial future will suffer. Remember, the grunts don't make any decisions, are the last to know what's going on, and usually are the first ones affected when the company experiences difficult financial times. If one grunt quits, there's always another grunt to take their place.

Remember, this is not industry-specific. I am in no way belittling anyone's chosen profession or occupation. There are many people with advanced degrees and prestigious titles who don't recognize (or don't mind) that they, too, are grunts. I was once a grunt – a pretty damn good one, if I must say.

But I moved on, and I changed my position.

Now, let's talk about why you need to do the same thing.

CHAPTER 9

CHANGE YOUR POSITION OR: *MOVE UP, NOT OVER*

Every industry expects the newcomers to "pay their dues" before they advance up the structure. To become a millionaire, you must do everything in your power to change your position and rise out of grunt-dom as quickly as possible.

In most sectors, the first step usually means becoming a manager, supervisor, director, or lead so-and-so. As I said earlier, moving up in your structure will usually come with some degree of monetary gain: As you advance, you'll find that your compensation will increase at a *much* faster rate than those below you.

And if you can work your way into the C-suite, your total compensation will greatly outpace inflation or any standard raise. The great thing about being in the C-suite is that your pay is not based on the amount of hours you put in or the quality of your work. It's all about your title. This happens in a wide variety of professions. In sports, a quarterback is usually the highest-paid player on a NFL team... even if he's not that productive or the best player.

But there's more to moving up than a one-time salary increase:

Your position determines who you get to spend time around, who you work with, and who you talk to.[50] The higher up you go, the more closely you will work with people shaping the company you work for. You'll see how they make decisions and understand the high-level challenges they face; challenges that you haven't experienced yourself. You'll also have the ability to influence decisions rather than being on the receiving end. You'll meet other key players in your industry: vendors, people who work for related companies or industries, those in unrelated industries, and so on. These key players can be a tremendous resource if you remember Rule #1: Be Teachable. Even if your company is successful, these outside players know sh*t you don't and have seen sh*t you haven't. In some ways, I've learned more valuable lessons from these individuals than anyone in my everyday circle.

All of this will be invaluable if you want to keep your momentum and keep climbing up the org chart. You will have to embrace changes and seek new opportunities. You'll need to recognize when you have to make your own changes and create your own opportunities.

And remember: You must move **UP**. This means you'll need to avoid falling into an endless cycle of lateral moves. These are not always easy to identify, and they are true career- and momentum-killers.

I see this a lot in my industry: Doctors move from Hospital A to Hospital B because Hospital B seems like a better opportunity. But when you dig a little deeper, they're doing the same job; working with the same kinds of people. They aren't acquiring new skills. They aren't gaining influence or establishing valuable new connections. For these people, a change of environment and a slight pay increase creates the illusion of change, but in reality it's often a case of *same sh*t, different hospital.*

50 For the grammar sticklers: The use of "who" in this sentence is technically incorrect. But "with whom you get to spend time" sounds a bit too formal for this book. And who the hell really talks like that?

This isn't unique to my field. It happens in every industry, from retail to construction to engineering to accounting. News anchors are notorious for jumping from one network to the next. However, they are not moving up their industry's structure. One day, they're doing the weather for Channel X; the next day, they're doing the weather for Channel Y.

In many cases, these people are chasing small raises. And while it's true that these lateral moves might provide them with several thousand dollars more per year, they're missing out on other potentially valuable opportunities. Eventually, they'll run out of lateral moves to make – and hospitals or TV stations or accounting firms to move to – and they won't have the skills, experience, or connections to go anywhere else.

To avoid this trap, you need to think carefully before making a change or moving to another place. Ask yourself if the position you're considering is any different from what you are currently doing. Will you be taking on new responsibilities? Learning new sh*t? Interacting with new, more influential people? Will the position move you closer to a long-term career goal?

Legendary college basketball coach John Wooden summed up my opinion of lateral moves in one powerful sentence.

I need to say this one more time: You will never develop additional skills and maximize your wealth-building potential by living a life made up of a continuous string of lateral moves. Assuming that you aren't miserable where you are and that you don't work with a bunch of a-holes, you're much better off trying to move up the ranks in one organization than hopping from place to place doing the same job in a different environment.

The funny thing is, if you're not lazy or an a-hole, you'll find that this is fairly easy to accomplish. It can be challenging to find dedicated, motivated people who care about the quality of their work and their professional growth - and this means that, if you're a quality employee, you will likely have the opportunity to move up within your organization's structure.

Here are some things you can do to make that happen:

- ✓ **FIGURE SH*T OUT.** Be a go-getter! I don't know how many times I've heard someone on the job complain that no one has trained or told them what to do. Be resourceful. Be proactive. Find ways to learn what you need.

- ✓ **INVEST IN YOUR EDUCATION.** Take at least 1% of your salary and use it to develop a new skill. For example, if you make $50k/year, make a commitment to spend a minimum of $500/year educating yourself. Sign up for an online or in-person course or seminar.

- ✓ **SOCIALIZE WITH YOUR CO-WORKERS AND COLLEAGUES.** Being perceived as likable most times outweighs any shortcoming you may have when it comes to your knowledge base and/or technical skill. People are more inclined to help those they like.

Of course, changing your position is not always possible in some structures. Your immediate supervisor, manager, or boss may not be going anywhere for a long time. You may be working for a small company with no real opportunities for growth.

If this applies to you, there are only two options:

1) **MAINTAIN THE STATUS QUO, AND START EDUCATING YOURSELF.** Look at your boss and your boss' boss: How did they get where they are? What skills do they have that helped them get there? What do you need to learn if you want to hold a similar position with another company?
2) **BRANCH OFF AND DO YOUR OWN THING.** As we discussed in Chapter 4, your skills are portable. At this point, you may decide to say F*CK IT – which, in this case, might mean taking your skills, experience, and expertise and doing something entirely new, like starting your own business, producing a product or service, etc.

MOVING ON... *BACK?*

If you are in a position where there is no room for advancement – whether you've gone as high up the ranks as you can, or there simply aren't any opportunities to advance with your particular skillset – you may need to step back, move down the corporate ladder, and maybe even take a pay cut in order to learn/grow/move.

There is nothing wrong with moving back a few steps in the pursuit of self-discovery, self-development, or career advancement. In some situations, a temporary move backwards will make you stronger in the end. The higher you go, the more likely it is that you'll run out of ways to move – so you might need to move down temporarily; spend some time on the sidelines while you grow and develop yourself.

Just be sure that you aren't making a lateral move. You won't learn anything that way.

CHAPTER 10

DON'T BECOME A HOSTAGE TO PAST SUCCESSES (OR FAILURES)

There are plenty of books and online articles that discuss the importance of embracing and dealing with failure. I think this goes back to our collective fascination with "underdog" stories: We like to hear about people who tried, failed, tried again, maybe failed again, but eventually succeeded.

These stories make us feel better. They're proof that, even if we fail, we might still overcome our eventual failures and find success - and that we shouldn't let things like our economic status, age, gender, ethnicity, or appearance hold us back or get in the way. Even if we fail, we should get up, dust ourselves off, and try again.

It's also important to understand *why* you failed, which can sometimes be painful. Nobody really likes reliving their failures. But financially speaking, you need to have a firm understanding of why you are not where you want to be monetarily. You need to understand how your past decisions and actions led you to your present situation.

As an emergency medicine physician, I was trained to objectively examine my patient care decisions, particularly the ones that resulted in an unanticipated patient outcome. The great thing about the medical community is that, if a patient has an unexpected negative outcome, your colleagues and the treating healthcare institution will look at the case on your behalf to see if you deviated from the standard of care. This can actually be quite stressful, depending on what happened to the patient, but the end result is worth it: These reviews can help create practices that hopefully eliminate the possibility of a repeat incident.

You must go through this same exact process with your financial failures. Did you trust the wrong person or invest in the wrong business? Did you buy too much of the wrong crap, marry the wrong person, pursue the wrong career, or do some combination of these?

Whether or not you have pain associated with your financial past, please understand and embrace the following:

Your past has determined your present, but your present will determine your future.

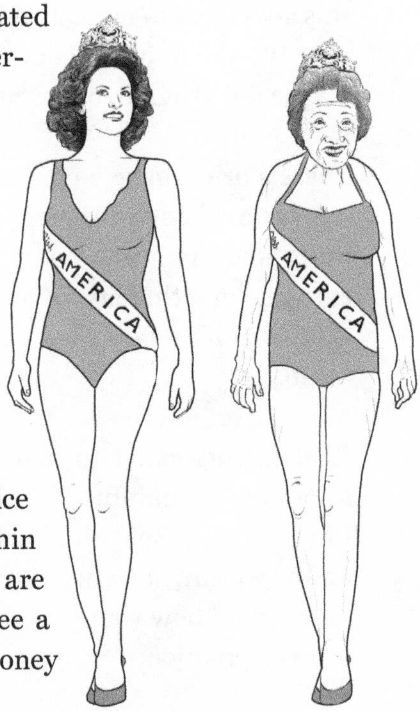

You must use whatever time you have in the present to correct financial mistakes from your past in order to have a better future. You definitely will not notice a change overnight. However, within a couple of years (assuming you are working), you should be able to see a measurable difference (i.e. more money in the bank).

You can't let your past failures hold you back.

That said, I think it's equally important that you don't become a hostage to your past successes, either. I've met too many people who take the attitude of, "Whew, I'm glad I made it this far. I'm finally doing X for a living, and I'm finally making $X per year. I'm done."

When you get too complacent, you lose your hunger to keep learning, keep moving up, and keep developing new skills. You lose your hustle. And if you lose your hustle, you're going to have a hard time becoming a millionaire.

After I completed high school, I was accepted to a well-regarded university based on the coursework I completed and the grades I received when I was between 15 and 17 years old. (That was a long time ago!) I spent my post-college/med school years working my way up in my field. I started out as a staff ER physician. From there, I moved up to assistant medical director, and, finally, medical director. While I'm proud of these accomplishments, I wasn't content to stop there. I viewed all of these things as past successes, and I knew that if I wanted to enjoy future success in my professional life, I needed to stay hungry – for knowledge, for skills, for new opportunities, for additional ways to increase my income. I couldn't lose my hustle just because I put an "M.D." after my name.

Someone who was Miss America in the 1960s, 70s, or 80s may have ruled the swimsuit competition back then, but it's likely that they have had to move on and develop other "skills" since then. (After all, there are only so many job opportunities for geriatric bikini models.)

Someone who was the star quarterback of their high school or college football team eventually had to find a job that provided a steady paycheck and less risk of concussion.

As a pre-wardrobe-malfunction Janet Jackson once asked, "What Have You Done For Me Lately?"

That sums up my point pretty succinctly. No one cares what you did 10-20 years ago. Hell, the world is moving so quickly that your work and achievements from two years ago don't matter much, either.

I have met Ivy League graduates who, based on their current life, look like they may have peaked in college or graduate school. They got a fancy degree from an impressive school, and they were content to coast through life without achieving much more. At the same time, I've met people who attended "no-name" colleges who have gone on to become multi-millionaires.

The difference is that the "no-name" graduates never lost their hustle.

What about you? What are you doing today to make your life and your financial situation better?

CHAPTER 11

OWNERSHIP IS KEY

Take a few moments to list everything you own.

If you're like most people, your list may look like this:

- ✓ Car
- ✓ House
- ✓ Stock investments
- ✓ Retirement accounts
- ✓ Personal effects (clothing, jewelry, etc.)

Now, think about your career and your ability to make money: Do you have ownership of anything that will help you grow your skills, advance your career, or bring in additional income? Do you have any ownership of the products and/or services you create?

The market rewards owners with a disproportionate amount of the financial gains derived from any business. At first glance, this may not seem quite fair – after all, the owner has employees who make the company possible and take care of all of the day-to-day tasks. Why do the employees make so little, comparatively speaking?

What's easy to forget, though, is that business owners are also the ones taking all the risks – especially in those precarious startup years. There's this idea out there that starting a business is a path to wealth. And, while it's true that entrepreneurship can create wealth, it's also incredibly risky. It's not all sunshine and rainbows and stacks of cash. I read somewhere that a little more than half of all new businesses fail within the first year. And of the ones that survive that first year, more than 90% of them go under in a decade.

And when a business goes under, the business owner is the one left to pick up the pieces, financially speaking. They are the ones who take the loss, file for bankruptcy, etc. Employees can just go find other jobs... provided, of course, that they have portable, desirable skills and haven't lost their hustle.

So, what do you *really* own? What are you creating for your company – and does it belong to you? Are you sharing in the reward?

If your answer is: "I don't own anything" or "I created X, but I am not sharing in the rewards," it's time that you start exploring your options.

A good place to start: **THE SIDE HUSTLE.**

What's a side hustle?

Well, here's what a side hustle is NOT:

- **IT'S NOT IDENTICAL TO YOUR CURRENT JOB.** Let's say you're a fry cook at Fast Food Restaurant A or a nurse anesthetist at Surgery Center A. Taking on hours as a fry cook at Fast Food Restaurant B or as a nurse anesthetist at Surgery

Center B is *NOT* a side hustle, it's a second job. And at the end of the day, you're still just making someone else wealthy.

- **IT'S NOT SOMETHING THAT WILL MAKE YOU A TON OF EXTRA CASH UP FRONT.** A side hustle isn't a get-rich-quick scheme.
- **IT'S NOT AN ALTERNATIVE TO YOUR 9-TO-5 JOB.** Most people will need the security (and steady income) from their current jobs as they pursue a side hustle.

Ideally, a side hustle is a separate venture that will eventually give you ownership of an idea, product, or service. Something that's *yours* – not your company's or your employer's.

When it comes to choosing your side hustle, you have three options:

1) **YOU CAN PURSUE DERIVATIVE WORK.** This is basically taking the skills you have and branching off to do your own thing. Let's say you're a construction manager for a commercial developer. You could start a side hustle by developing and building a custom single-family home. Although the commercial and residential markets are different, the skillsets needed for success are very similar. You just need to learn the nuances – the slight differences in clientele, processes, and terminology – between the two.

2) **YOU CAN DO SOMETHING ENTIRELY NEW.** This option involves a bit more risk because you're entering completely uncharted territory, skills- and career-wise. If you are interested in going this route, I suggest you keep the following in mind: First of all, it's critical that you aren't basing your choice solely on how much money you think you can make. You might have a friend who is making

a killing in real estate – but if you have zero interest in real estate, don't even consider it. If you don't have a true passion or vision for this new venture, you will not have the wherewithal to make it through those difficult times. Not sure what kind of new venture is right for you? Take a look back at the list of intelligence types in Chapter 3. If you're going to branch off and do something new, you need to make sure the universe (through genetic predisposition) is aligned with you.

3) **YOU CAN JOIN SOMEONE ELSE'S SIDE HUSTLE.** Between work and everything else in your life, you may not have enough time, money, or talent to pursue your first side hustle on your own. And that's okay. For a first-time venture, it's okay if you end up – at least initially – with less than 100% ownership of something. Hell, even a 5% or 10% ownership of something is a good start. Find someone pursuing something that you find interesting or exciting (and preferably something that aligns with your skills or intelligence type), and join forces with them. Just remember that you need to bring something of value to the partnership (a unique skill or background, financial resources, connections and networking opportunities, and/or energy). If you don't bring value, you're just adding dead weight to the project – and eventually, someone is going to vote you off the island.

Remember, a side hustle is not a replacement for your job. And, if you're like most people, your life is already pretty damn busy.

Again: **The importance of having a decent paying job or a steady income cannot be more passionately emphasized.**

Unless you are part of a (very lucky) minority out there who can get by on a spouse's income or make do with family money while they get a side hustle going, you are going to need to have a steady job with decent income. I define this as any job where you earn enough to cover your basic living expenses, with some left over to save.

Before you seriously consider a side hustle, I suggest that you examine your current financial situation. Do you have an income problem? Equally important: Do you have a spending problem? I know I'm guilty of having bought clothes I haven't worn, gym memberships I haven't used, and premium cable channels I haven't watched.[51] Sometimes it's easier to save the money you have than make more of it. It's hard (damn near impossible, really) to start a side hustle unless you have money saved up or available to fund it.

Mind you, I'm not necessarily talking about a tremendous amount of money. Even if it took you a few years, could you save $5,000? Maybe you already have $5,000. Depending on what you wanted to do as your side hustle, $5,000 may be enough to start. For those of you thinking that $5,000 is not going to change your life, think about this: It sure as hell did for Sara Blakely, the founder and owner of Spanx. She took her life savings of $5,000 to create a product and company that has made her a billionaire.

Don't have $5,000? How much can you come up with?

Of course, if your side hustle is creative work, you may be able to get started with much less up-front cash. If you are a writer, for example, you really just need a laptop, an Internet connection, and a few hours a day of writing time. When J.K. Rowling created the fictional world of Harry Potter, she was on welfare

51 The only exception to this is HBO during "Game of Thrones" season.

benefits – so I'm assuming she had very little, if any, disposable cash.

What's my point in saying all of this? A side hustle is a great option – and if you pick the right one and go about it the right way, a side hustle can become a viable source of income.

Take a few minutes and do some brainstorming. Use the boxes below to write down at least three ideas for a potential side hustle.

SIDE HUSTLE IDEA #1	SIDE HUSTLE IDEA #2	SIDE HUSTLE IDEA #3

A FINAL NOTE ON SIDE HUSTLES: THE STOCK MARKET

You may have noticed by now that I haven't said much about the stock market. The main reason for that is that, if you want standard financial advice about stocks, you won't find it here. This isn't that kind of finance book.

As I've already told you, I am a big fan of the stock market. I like the idea that you can invest money in your favorite company and/or mutual fund and, over the course of many years, watch your money grow significantly.

But I'm *NOT* going to tell you to invest X% of your income in the stock market. Although I love the market, I am also aware that the stock market is not a good fit for everyone, and it does pose some challenges that make it difficult for the average person to build significant wealth in their lifetime:

1) **IT'S UNPREDICTABLE.** Investing in stocks is the riskiest thing you could ever do if you decided to invest for only 1 year. That may be the year that the market crashes. Accurate timing is critical over such a short period of time. What makes the market a relatively safe investment is that over a long period of time (10+ years), you shouldn't lose money. If all goes well, you should have made at least 7% per year on your money. Those who started investing in 2009 (post-financial crisis) have nothing but positive experiences with the market. However, at some point, as any "Game of Thrones" fan will tell you, winter always comes!

2) **IT'S INCOME-DEPENDENT.** The more money you earn, the more money you have left over to invest. You've seen those projections of how much money you would have

in 30 years if you just invested $1,000 per month. Well, what happens if you only have $20 or $50 per month to invest? If you're just trying to make ends meet, you don't have any money to risk in the market.

3) **IT DOESN'T IMPROVE YOUR CURRENT LIFESTYLE.** The way the market delivers the best return is when you put the money in and don't touch it for a few decades. You can look at your growing account balance, but you're not supposed to withdraw the money for many years. This reminds me of being a kid and going to my grandmother's house. Her beautiful living room furniture was off-limits to my cousins and me. It was eternally covered with some form of durable see-through plastic so it wouldn't get damaged by us kids. We could look at the furniture from a distance and admire its beauty, but we could not touch it. You are not supposed to use your stock market money until it's had years to mature and compound – which, in many of our cases, won't be until we're old and gray. That's no fun. I want to buy a jet ski now, not when I'm 70. Also, what happens if I don't make it to retirement?

CHAPTER 11.2

HOW I STARTED MY SIDE HUSTLE

In case you were wondering, I'm not just giving you empty advice when it comes to ownership and side hustles. A major factor in my ability to become a millionaire was my decision to branch out, take a risk, and create my own business. Well, it wasn't exclusively "my" business: I had partners;[52] we were all equal owners; and we each contributed money, time, and effort to getting our business off the ground.

Here's how it started:

About six years into my career as an emergency physician, I began to realize that I wasn't living the life I wanted. I was on the treadmill of life and needed a way to get off. I was expected to see and move patients through the ER at roughly the same speed as a UPS worker might sort and process boxes through a distribution center.

Anyone who has been to an emergency room knows there's

52 I don't just provide words of wisdom, I follow my own advice: My first side hustle involved partners. I was much too busy (and much too risk-averse) to strike out on my own.

always a long wait. By the time the patient got called back to a room, they were usually pretty frustrated after having waited for so long. As the doctor on duty, I would get frustrated as well: I knew that, if not for the inefficiencies in the hospital system, the patient could have been brought back much sooner for treatment. Who wants to work in an environment where people are not only sick and/or injured, but also start off their care somewhat dissatisfied? It's a helpless feeling that can best be understood by those working in the ER trenches throughout America.

To add insult to injury, I also recognized that I didn't really have any ownership working in the hospital ER. My ER group's contract was only good as long as the hospital administrator's level of satisfaction was high. It took me six years too long to realize that I was basically working in a dead-end job. Here's the funny thing: I wasn't the only one of my colleagues who felt that way. Each of us was miserable in our own unique way. So we decided to do something about. Seven other physicians and I joined forces to start our own emergency center. This is a good example of **DERIVATIVE WORK**: My colleagues and I took our existing skills and branched off to create something that we owned.

Of course, it's important to note that this is something that the laws in Texas allowed us to do. If I lived in any other state, this wouldn't have been possible. Remember what I said in Chapter 5 about needing the government's help in order to accumulate wealth? At the time we started our side hustle, the law in Texas[53] – in other words, *the government* – allowed non-hospital entities to operate stand-alone emergency centers.

53 This is somewhat unique, and Texas is one of only three or four states that allow this.

As is common with many new businesses, our early years were a struggle. This was compounded by the fact that several of my partners lost their jobs at the hospital because our new ER center was viewed as a competitive threat. We also needed to take out several joint loans[54] for over $1 million to get the business off the ground. I was working 96 hours (for free!) each month to get the emergency center off the ground, and then putting in another 160-180 hours per month at the hospital to pay the bills.

After almost three years in business, we finally got our feet underneath us and became profitable. What started as one center in our first year grew to five centers three years later, nine centers the year after that, and then 18 centers the following year.

Looking back on our success, some may say we all just got lucky. While there was probably a bit of luck involved, I prefer to view it as a situation where preparation met opportunity. We didn't know exactly what we were doing in the beginning, but because we had the skills (we were ER physicians) to provide the service and the money (from stable, good-paying jobs and the bank) to take the risk, the universe rewarded us with a successful business.

As I mentioned earlier, the key aspect to keep in mind is that *I actually owned a portion of the business* where I was providing the service. I wasn't just an employee. By taking the initial risk, I was rewarded with a portion of the profits that far surpassed what I could earn as someone working for hourly wages only.

54 The eight of us signed up for the loan jointly; however, if seven of us died, the one remaining guy would be responsible for the whole loan.

More importantly, the business was able to deliver its service (emergency care) without me having to be there all the time – which left me with enough time to do other things (like develop my skills, pursue other opportunities, read books, and attend conferences, to name a few).

CHAPTER 12

YOU WILL BE DEAD SOMEDAY

In my career in emergency medicine, I've witnessed at least 100 people die, including several children. To me, death is not some abstract concept or remote eventuality. It is very real. In a fraction of a second, your life could be over.

Yes, I know that's some sobering sh*t.

For those of you who may be a little more sensitive, this may sound kind of depressing. What's the point in working hard, just to have it all come to an end at any moment?

Here's how I choose to see it: My life is going to come to an end at some point. That being the case, I choose to view every day I have on Earth as a gift. I believe that time is my most valuable asset, and I want to be the one who decides how I spend the time I have.

Your time is finite. The more time that goes by, the less time you have left to become a millionaire.

Country singer Tim McGraw said it best:

So, how do you make the most of the time you have?

I suggest you start by asking yourself this simple question: "If I keep doing X, what will my life look like three, five, or 10 years from now?"

This is the question I asked myself as a 29-year-old ER doctor – a "grunt" working alongside docs who had been doing the job for 10 years or more. I liked to think they were once young, energetic, bright-eyed, and bushy-tailed just like me. However, 10 to 15 years later, they were no longer energetic, bright-eyed, or bushy-tailed. They were slow and tired. They were just getting through the day. To me, they seemed resigned to the fact that this is how their life would be; they'd be toiling away in the ER until they retired or died or got laid off and replaced by younger people willing to work for less money.

Of course, there were a few who were just trying to coast by doing the minimum necessary to keep their jobs. But these people were in the minority. Most of these docs were giving it their best effort, but the effects of Father Time had taken hold. They simply didn't have the stamina or the tolerance to do the job.

Four years into my career, I looked over at a fellow ER doc and said, "We're *not* doing this when we're 40."

He rolled his eyes and told me to shut up (we'd known each other since high school), and we went back to work.

At that moment, though, I made an internal declaration that I wanted my life to be different. I didn't know what I wanted to be doing in 10 years. I didn't know what I should do next, what position I should aspire to, or how to get there. But I knew that I needed to work toward a change - and that was enough to get me started. The thought of being in the ER at 40 years old was enough to push me to start looking at my options and considering all of the possibilities.

It's kind of like being in an unsatisfying relationship. You aren't happy. You know that the person you're with is not the person you want to be with long-term. And you know that staying with that person for another three, five, or 10 years isn't going to change anything. You might not know who you want your partner to be. You might be alone for the rest of your life, or you just might find the right person in a few months. But you reach the point where an uncertain future is better than an unhappy present.

You need to learn to look at your career and financial situation the same way you'd look at an unsatisfying relationship. What does the future look like if you stay where you are for the next several years? If you're still young, take a look at the older people in your company or profession – people who were doing your job a decade ago: What are they doing now? Where did their skills take them? If you're older, look at what people in your industry ended up doing prior to exiting stage left. Have any of these people had interesting second careers post-retirement?

No matter how old you are, you should make sure to ask yourself this critical question: *Have I Missed My Window of Opportunity?*

Unfortunately, life is not a Disney movie. Just because you want something really desperately, doesn't mean you will achieve it if you only work harder. Remember, the market determines the value of your skills – and certain skills have a finite shelf-life.

If you are a great athlete, your career will be over by your 40th birthday.[55] I am actually being generous when I say this because most athletic careers end at ages 25-26. If you are a 23-year-old pro football player, it's high time you started thinking about what your life will look like in five years. This is the difference between athletes who are successful later in life and those who end up broke and desperate. The successful ones know that they only have a finite number of years in them – and they start exploring their options early on. These are the guys[56] who take their skills and knowledge and go on to have successful careers as coaches or sportscasters. Some, like Kevin Plank,[57] use their experience to develop better equipment or clothing.

---

55 If you look hard enough, you can probably find the odd 44-year-old Major League Baseball player or 45-year-old professional hockey star. But these guys are the exception to the rule and certainly NOT the norm.

56 And, to a certain extent, ladies – although women's professional sports still tend to take a backseat to men's. If this pisses you off (and it's understandable if it does), this is a good opportunity to "criticize by creating." Coach girls' sports. Buy tickets to WNBA games.

57 See p. 97

I find it kind of shocking that we still have guys like Latrell Sprewell and former NFL quarterback, Vince Young who seem completely unprepared for life after professional sports. What did they expect? Did they think it was a coincidence that none of their teammates was over 35 years old?

It's also an unfortunate truth that some goals have shelf-lives, too. If you are in your 30s and still hoping to become a professional football or baseball player, you need to start exploring other options. Depending on your skillset, you might even be able to find a career that is still related to sports – like sports marketing, sports reporting, becoming an agent, or sports medicine.

I'm not just picking on athletes here: By the time you hit your 30s, you are also unlikely to become a successful rock star. Mind you, this is not because you lack talent – but the simple fact is that most successful musical acts rely on audiences composed of people in their teens and 20s – people who have the free time to discover new music and who can go to weeknight shows. If you're 35+ and still trying to make it in the music industry as a performer, you need to be aware that your target audience is busy working, raising kids, etc. They don't have the time to develop a passion or cult-like following for your music.

That sounds harsh. Please note that I don't want to kill your dream, but rather refocus it.

Here's a test: If you must run, jump, sing, dance, lift heavy objects, climb tall heights, crawl in tight spaces, function on less than five hours of sleep, look young and beautiful, or see 40 patients in one shift to make your money, the writing is on the wall.

What do you do next? How do you refocus your goals?

First, you need to . . .

UNDERSTAND WHERE YOU ARE IN YOUR LIFE'S TIMELINE

I'm convinced that the whole world has a case of Peter Pan syndrome. You've heard the statements: "40 is the new 30!" or "50 is the new 40!"

People aren't defining "old age" in the same way anymore. Today's older people are more sophisticated and tech-savvy than previous generations of older people. They text and send emails (although those emails are often chain letters written in ALL CAPS); they retire later; they have smartphones and tablet computers; they stay active (physically and – given the amount of commercials for Viagra and whatnot – sexually too).

At the same time, though, most 50-year-olds are NOT out clubbing until 2 a.m. Thursday night and waking up at 7:30 a.m. so they can get to work by 9 a.m. on Friday. They're not lining up to take extra overtime shifts. They're not scoring touchdowns or landing million-dollar modeling contracts. They're not starting businesses or aggressively working their way up the corporate ladder. And, in my experience, they are at a point in life where they don't want to take a lot of risks. They are too busy saving for retirement or putting their kids through college. They have more to lose, financially speaking.

As we age, we do not physically recover as quickly as we did in our younger years. I never bought into the idea that age is just a state of mind. The average American still dies sometime in their mid-to-late 70s. And it's not like those people are perfectly healthy at age 76 until they just drop dead one day. People may be living longer, but in their last few years, their lives usually revolve around doctors' appointments, hospitalizations, and remembering to take their umpteen medications.

It is highly unlikely that you will be motivated - or have the energy - to work hard, particularly for financial gain, when you are in your 70s or 80s. Please note, I am NOT saying that you should give up on starting a business or pursuing a lifelong career goal if you are over 50. But I AM saying that it's important to be realistic. I suggest surrounding yourself with younger people who have the energy, stamina, and knowhow to help with the heavy lifting.

And, most importantly, you need to surround yourself with people who are young enough to put up with all of the bullsh*t.

The older you get, the more important this will become.

When I was younger, I was puzzled by those stories about older couples who divorce after 20 or 30 years together. *Why now?* I'd wonder. *Why bother divorcing after that much time?*

Now that I'm older, I think I get it: When you get older, you are less willing to put up with bullsh*t. You are less willing to work at jobs where you can't move up or learn new skills. You are less interested in spending time with people who treat you poorly. I figure that's the case with these couples who divorce after decades: Someone in that relationship finally hit their bullsh*t breaking point.

Remember what dating was like when you were in your 20s? You probably put up with your share of bullsh*t for a lot longer than you'd be willing to put up with today.

Why? Because . . .

YOUR ABILITY TO TOLERATE BULLSH*T IS INVERSELY PROPORTIONAL TO YOUR AGE.

If you're more of a visual person, the graph below illustrates how our tolerance for bullsh*t decreases as we get older:

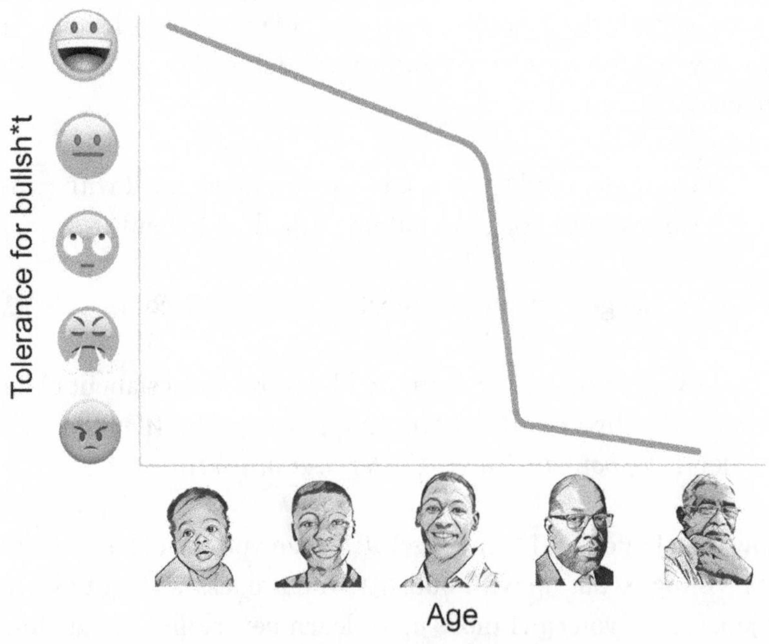

In addition to losing our tolerance for bullsh*t as we age, we also become more inflexible and less adaptable – "set in our ways," as the saying goes. Unfortunately, this also means we become *MUCH* less teachable. We are less willing to humble ourselves and admit that there is still some sh*t out there that we don't know.

If I may quote Socrates for a moment,

Most people in their 40s and 50s would never call themselves know-it-alls, although they sometimes act and behave like they do know it all. Maybe it's because this is the age when we start feeling our mortality; when the idea that you will be dead someday really starts to sink in. We see our time as increasingly valuable, and we are less willing to use that time admitting that we don't know something or letting a younger person teach us something.

On the other hand, people in their 20s or 30s might feel like they have all the time in the world. Sure, they'll be dead someday – but *WAY* in the future. Right now, it's all about the present. Why worry now?

When I was a 19-year-old college student, I would do damn near anything for money – as long as it wasn't illegal. I signed up for who-knows-how-many research studies at my university, where I'd spend two weeks as a guinea pig, eating questionable foods or taking salt pills or sleeping with a bunch of wires and sh*t taped to my chest to monitor my heart rate.[58] Now that I'm a physician, I think I was insane to take a pill and not really understand the potential effects, just for a quick payday. Back then, though, I needed the money, and I was happy to do it – at the end of the two weeks, I'd get $500 or so. That was more money than I'd ever made at one time! I'd put up with just about any form of bullsh*t if it meant a few hundred bucks in my pocket.

Would I do something like that *today* for $500?

Hell, no. I don't need $500 that badly. And as a parent, there's no way I'd let my daughters do something like that.[59]

So, where are you in your life's timeline? Are you in the late adolescence/early adulthood stage of "I'll-do-anything-for-cash-as-long-as-it's-legal"? Have you moved into a much-more-caution, much-less-clubbing middle age? Are you heading to your "no bullsh*t" golden years?

Once you know where you are in your life's timeline, here's your next step:

TAKE A LOOK AT YOUR ENTIRE COMPANY OR INDUSTRY.

---

58 It's funny but also kind of scary when I reflect on that experience. There's an expression that God looks out for the young, the old, and the dumb. At the time, two of these applied.

59 The funny thing is that, in my efforts to protect them from the possible side effects of weird food and salt pills, I might be hurting their ability to develop certain character traits, like the ability to hustle. While somewhat risky, my years of doing almost anything for money did help me develop a strong work ethic and a sense of self-reliance. On some level, I might be discouraging them from developing an adventurous, no-holds-barred mentality. By being a good provider as a father, I am simultaneously destroying their hustler mentality. I'll get into this more in the next chapter, but the unfortunate truth is that parents often stifle their children's dreams and abilities one way or another.

What kinds of jobs are people your age doing? How about people 5, 10, or even 15 years older than you? What opportunities are available as you age? Who are the people who make the most money in your industry? Where are they in their lives' timeline?

Everyone wants to be the star. The media showers the star with all the praise and attention. But if you look at things more broadly, the "star" in your industry may or may not be the person who makes the most money. Here's an example: In the National Football League, the "stars" - in this case, the players - make a lot of money. But the overwhelming majority don't make as much money as the NFL commissioner. This is the guy who probably never played professional *OR* college football. But he brings home a salary higher than most players in the league.

It's a pretty sweet deal: The NFL commissioner doesn't have to participate in any drills, and he doesn't have to memorize playbooks. He's not at risk for a concussion (on the field, that is); and he probably doesn't think about pulling a hamstring, turf toe, high ankle sprains, or tearing his ACL. The same could be said about the NBA commissioner (minus the turf toe).

Remember, don't hate the player, hate the game.

This is why, although the idea of being a "star" *sounds* awesome, it's usually better, financially speaking, to be the person who is behind the scenes pulling the strings. Physical talent ALWAYS fades, but mental talent can carry you through your entire lifetime.

The most successful people are those who learn this early and figure out how to transfer their talents, skills, and abilities to some other opportunity.

Barbara Walters is a great example of someone who did this. In a field rampant with gender discrimination and double standards about age, she has remained relevant. She has accomplished this by using her talents, skills, and experience to break off and do her own thing. In an age where it's hard to find a (female) news anchor over 30, you can still catch 80-something, semi-retired Barbara on TV now and then.

I find stories like hers inspiring. I like to imagine it all starting with 25-year-old Barbara asking herself, interview-style, "If I keep doing this job, where will I be in five years?"

I still ask myself that question.

And maybe it's because of my time in the ER, but the other question I tend to ask myself is, "When I'm on my deathbed, is this going to matter to me?"

This is why I left a six-figure job as a Chief Medical Officer. I imagined being on my deathbed, regretting how much time I spent in pointless meetings, discussing the same five or six issues with the same people in the same damn office and getting nowhere. It wasn't that my role and responsibilities weren't important, but I wasn't growing. I was spending the majority of my time managing and developing other people and/or processes, but I wasn't developing *me*. Most importantly, dealing with the a-holes around me was literally sucking the life and creativity out of me. I knew that, if I kept that job, I wouldn't have the life I wanted.

Forget five years. I couldn't imagine staying at that job for another five months. So, I quit.[60]

60 Mind you, this isn't the first time that I quit a somewhat coveted and lucrative job. I came to the same conclusion four years into my medical director position. I was no longer growing. So I had to leave. This was another six-figure job I just let go. I wasn't technically a millionaire back then, but didn't need this position to make ends meet.

Being a millionaire gave me the freedom to walk away.

I don't know exactly what I am going to do next. My immediate goal was to write this book and share what I'd learned in the hopes that others could learn and also benefit from my experience. But I'm not going to stop growing, learning, and developing.

I don't want you to think that I made a cavalier or impulsive decision by leaving my job. Nothing could be further from the truth. What may have appeared as a sudden change to others happened somewhat according to my plan. Making decisions in a willy-nilly fashion would be a disgrace to my fellow INTJ brethren. I didn't take this time off to finally watch "Breaking Bad" or engage in some other Quadrant 4 leisure activity. There's still a lot of sh*t I want to learn and a lot of things I still want to do. For example, I love animated movies, and I have a pipe dream about making a Pixar-quality type film.

This is why, when I enjoy a movie, I usually sit through the credits to see who the executive producers, producers, and directors were. I then record their names and research them on the Internet. If they have written any books, I read them. I've read Pixar co-founder Ed Catmull's book, "Creativity Inc.: Overcoming the Unseen Forces that Stand in the Way of True Inspiration." This is also why I watch animated films not necessarily for their entertainment value, but to learn the art of effective storytelling. I've even taken a couple of screenwriting classes.

Where will I be in five years? I don't know. But I know where I *won't* be.

And for now, that's enough.

I'll be dead someday. So will you. We can't do anything about that – but we can make the most of the time we have.

CHAPTER 13

IDENTIFY YOUR NETWORK

If someone isn't doing something productive with their life, it is highly unlikely that they will add anything or produce anything positive in your life

I got a call recently from a former coworker who had been a few rungs down from me on the corporate ladder at my last job. She's getting to that point in her career where she can't see herself doing the same thing for another five or 10 years. She's ready to move on but doesn't know how. She doesn't even know what she wants to do. But she's got kids to take care of, so she can't just go on sabbatical or take a few months off to figure things out.

She wanted to know what she should do next.

The first thing I asked her was, "Well, who's the most successful person you know?"

"Well... I guess *you* are," she said.

She called me because she saw me as a role model. And, as part of her network, I was also someone she could reach out to for advice and ideas about how to use her skills and experience to move on to a job that was more challenging – and one that offered more opportunities for growth and for making money.

Who can you reach out to for career advice? Who is in your network?

Before you answer that, let's define what I mean by "network."

To me, "network" means the people you spend the majority of your time with, both personally and professionally. Your network is not static, but rather a living, breathing organism that can grow or shrink throughout your life.[61]

Most networks are made up of three prongs: family, friends, and associates. Some of them are more helpful than others.

Let's look at each in more detail.

FAMILY

Your family is your first network, and it is the network that lays the foundations and helps determine the likelihood of your future successes – or failures.

Do you come from a family of millionaires or multi-millionaires?

Does anyone in your family have a multi-million-dollar skill (as in, a skill that the market has decided is worth millions of dollars)?

Is your family networked with any millionaire families?

61 Your network is NOT your hundreds or thousands of Facebook friends or Twitter followers. These individuals do very little to help you grow your income and/ or skills. The only online social network that I consider useful in that capacity is LinkedIn, which was created precisely to help people identify and expand their networks.

I went to college with a lot of wealthy kids. And I mean *really* wealthy. These were the kids of world-famous high-end clothing designers, award-winning soap opera stars, vice-presidents, and other highly influential and very well-connected people. I was surrounded by 19- and 20-year-olds with entirely different lifestyles than mine. As a result, they had entirely different experiences and expectations about life, education, and success.

I didn't run in the same circles as most of the celebrity kids – but I still had plenty of friends who came from wealth. This really hit home for me during my junior year. A friend of mine – I'll call her Ashley[62] – was venting to me after having had a huge fight with her parents. I don't remember what the fight was about, but it was big enough and serious enough that Ashley's parents had cut her off financially. They were no longer paying for her tuition or her room and board. She was on her own.

To me, this sounded like a death sentence.

"That sucks! What are you going to do?" I asked.

Ashley shrugged. "I'll just have to pay for it myself."

I immediately went into problem-solving mode: "There are all kinds of loans you can apply for," I said. "There are work-study programs, grants..."

"No, I have my own money," she said. "My grandparents left it to me. I'll be fine."

To me, "paying for school" meant scraping by on a combination of loans, grants, scholarships, and part-time jobs. I was trying to be a good friend by offering Ashley solutions that made sense

62 Not her real name.

to me. As a kid from a working-class background, these are the solutions that made sense to me.

To Ashley, though, "paying for school" meant writing a check for $12,000 every semester... from her own bank account. When she said that she had her own money, she meant that she had more than enough money in the bank.

She wasn't even out of college, but my 19-year-old friend had already achieved what many middle-class people spend decades trying to achieve.

When I went to my 20-year college reunion, most of the wealthy kids – the kids like Ashley – had gone on to be wealthy adults. One guy ran his own hedge fund. Another started his own technology company. There were several people there who worked as private equity investors.

None of this was surprising, though. Most of my classmates came from wealthy families. To them, making boatloads of money was as natural as breathing. They were born into a pre-existing network of wealth.

Most of us don't come into the world with those kinds of advantages. If you're like me and the majority of other people, you did not grow up in a family that had the knowledge or access needed to become millionaires.

If you were lucky, your family was loving and supportive and encouraged you to pursue an education or a career – even if that led you down a path that was very different from anything that they'd experienced.

If you weren't lucky, your family's values, beliefs, and habits made for a hostile environment where your dreams and goals were undermined. If you grew up in a family like that, you were likely to hear things like:

> *"What the hell do you want to go to college for?"*
> *"Nobody in this family has ever amounted to anything."*
> *"You think you're better than us? Who do you think you are?"*

This is why I believe that *PARENTS ARE USUALLY THE REAL DREAM KILLERS.*

Unfortunately, as human beings, we're hardwired to put up with all manner of B.S. from our parents. When friends talk to us like that, we typically give them one - *maybe* two - chances to redeem themselves before we write them off as a-holes. But when a parent (or step-parent or guardian) tells us that we should just give up and that we won't ever amount to anything, we tend to listen and internalize it until we begin to believe it.

When we're kids, we hear our parents, teachers, and society in general telling us that we have to choose our friends carefully; that hanging out with the "wrong" crowd can set us up for failure, etc. The logic behind this centuries-old advice is that associating with the wrong peer group often determines the trajectory of your life. In other words, having "bad" friends doesn't only mess up your life now, but also shatters your chances for a brighter future.

While there might be some truth to this, I believe that this line of thinking greatly understates the role that your relationship with your family - particularly your parents - plays in the outcome of your life.

Here's an example: Over the course of my career, any time I've encountered patients who are dealing with deeply rooted psychological pain and dysfunction, the source is never a broken friendship. In 99.9% of these cases, the damage can be traced back to the family from which they came.

As you progress along your millionaire journey, you may encounter the greatest resistance from your parents or parental figures. If they are not millionaires, they may perceive your dreams, desires, and actions as delusions of grandeur. If you come from a very academic-oriented family, your artistic and creative dreams may garner little support. If you come from a family mired in generational poverty, a college degree or successful career may seem like a pipe dream. If you come from a very religious family, the pursuit of wealth may be viewed as being ungodly.

But remember: What your parents believe doesn't matter. Your parents don't determine the value of your desires and skills – the market does. As long as you are pursuing something that brings personal satisfaction, is (hopefully) legal, AND has tangible financial value, you should keep striving towards that goal.

And start widening your network and surrounding yourself with people who will help you pursue your chosen path.

FRIENDS

You can't choose your family, but you can definitely choose your friends. But can your friends help you work toward your goal of becoming a millionaire?

Maybe. That depends on the answers to these questions:

> *Is any one of your friends a millionaire or actively working toward that goal?*

Do any of your friends come from a family of millionaires? Are any of your friends networked to any millionaires?

I've learned that people use the word "friend" rather indiscriminately, regardless of the depth and/or length of the relationship with the other person.

In my world, there are three broad groups of "friends":

A) **LIFELONG FRIENDS.** These people are like family to you. They call you on your birthday, they're usually in your wedding party, and they can sleep at your house when they come into town and vice versa. Your families plan vacations together. They pretty much know all the key individuals in your personal life. No matter where you move, these friends will always keep in touch. This type of friendship is usually formed in childhood/late adolescence when you were most open to and trusting of people. Most importantly, these relationships were not founded with any intention of financial gain.

B) **SHARED-ENVIRONMENT FRIENDS.** This group is composed of people that you meet through your life and with whom you spend a fair amount of time. You typically make these friends via shared environments like school, work, church, or neighborhood. You may share meals, go to movies, or partake in other social events together. They may or may not know your birthday, but if they forget, it doesn't affect your friendship. They may or may not know your kids' names. You enjoy spending time with these friends when you are together, but once you are no longer a part of the same shared environment, you may eventually just "lose touch". These friendships are also not based on financial advancement.

C) **ASSOCIATES.** The people in this group are individuals you may or may not enjoy being around on a regular basis, but need in order to help you complete a given task or series of tasks (like starting a business). Most of the activities you engage in with this group are focused on accomplishing the task – and 85% to 95% of your conversations with these people will be related to that task. These people may or may not take the time to get to know you on a very personal level. Most importantly, people in this group have varying degrees of loyalty to you as a person. Some may be complete a-holes.[63] But that's okay. You don't have to like them, you just need to be able to work with them to accomplish the task. It's like they say in "The Godfather": *It's not personal. It's strictly business.*

Do any of your friend groups fulfill the questions I asked earlier?

If not, then you need to consider expanding your network of friends if you are serious about becoming a millionaire. For those of you who are in high school, college, or graduate school, let me share some advice that I wish someone had told me when I was in your position: The people you meet in school will come from a variety of backgrounds. A good majority of them will have been groomed very differently than you by their parents, communities, and experiences. This grooming may put them at a competitive advantage not only in school, but also in life.

Unfortunately, academic environments foster a spirit of competition rather than collaboration. Rather than seeing your classmates as people you may learn from, they are often viewed as people you need to outdo or outperform.

Sometimes, I regret not spending more time getting to know some of my wealthier classmates: the kids of celebrities or the

63 We'll talk more about the benefit of learning to deal with a-holes in Chapter 15.

kids who came from ultra-elite boarding schools like Phillips Exeter Academy or Phillips Academy Andover. I'm not sure if we would have become lifelong friends, but I probably could have learned a lot from them, simply because they were from a completely different environment than me. Of course, this wouldn't have been easy. When I wasn't studying, I was at the work-study job that helped me pay for my tuition. The wealthy students were going out and doing things and socializing – engaging in activities that helped them build their network. I didn't have that kind of time. And even if I'd had more leisure time, I probably wouldn't have chosen to spend it socializing. I'm an introvert by nature.

Remember that you never know who you are going to meet – at school, at work, at a volunteer gig, you name it. And you never know what they can teach you and what goals they can help you reach. Stay open-minded!

CHAPTER 14

WHO ARE YOUR FINANCIAL MENTORS?

When I was younger, I believed that a mentor had to be someone who personally took you under their wing and showed you everything you needed to know to succeed in life. They helped you improve a skill or become a better person, or they helped you develop some kind of code for living. Think Obi-Wan Kenobi (or Yoda) and Luke Skywalker; Professor Dumbledore and Harry Potter; Mr. Miyagi and Daniel LaRusso.

I have since learned that this is, well, *unrealistic.*

Unless you are a budding Jedi, a student wizard, or the Karate Kid, it's unlikely that you are going to find one person to act as your mentor and hold your hand as you figure sh*t out in life. That's just not how things work in the real world.

But this doesn't mean that you can't find mentors and role models who can help you develop your skills and work toward your goals. If you're very lucky, you might find a traditional mentor – a teacher or professor, a family member, or a supervisor at work you admire and who is willing to invest time in showing you the ropes. But even if you do have a person like that in your life, it's likely to be a finite relationship that fizzles once you graduate, move to a new city, or change jobs.

This is why it's important to look to other sources and become more flexible in your definition of "mentor." Despite what pop culture tells us, in many cases, our greatest mentoring relationships are completely one-sided; your greatest mentors may turn out to be people you never meet or interact with; people who will never know you exist.

And that's absolutely fine. Some of my greatest mentors are people I have never met. Hell, I'm not even sure if they would be people I would *like*, or vice versa. However, I've read their books - sometimes more than once - and I've gotten something useful out of them. Books are extremely helpful because they provide you with direct insight into a person's thoughts, life, and experiences. This is a very powerful thing. Someone who may not be interested or available to have a 30-second conversation with me will spend hundreds of pages talking about themselves and how they, their organizations, relationships, etc. became great.

To me, reading about how other people became wealthy is fun and exciting. At the end of this book, I have included several books that have helped me transform my way of thinking and, therefore, my life.

Stephen Covey[64] said, "The person who *doesn't* read is no better off than the person who *can't* read." But if you don't like to read, all is not lost.[65] Thanks to advances in technology, there

64 Yes, again with Stephen Covey. I consider Stephen Covey to be one of my financial mentors.

65 It's funny: When I was a kid, I *hated* reading. This is because, back then, I wasn't reading for academic enrichment or enjoyment, but rather to get a good grade on a test. Gulliver's Travels, Macbeth, Wuthering Heights, and The Canterbury Tales, may be great literary works, but they were b-o-r-i-n-g as hell. Back then, if you really wanted to torture me, you could just force me to read James Joyce, and I

are many shortcuts you can take to obtain the same information. Audiobooks and podcasts are great options – and they're ways to make your daily commute or hour on the treadmill productive.

The point is, whether you prefer to read books, listen to audiobooks or podcasts, or watch Internet videos, you can find works that inspire you, created by people you admire and think of as mentors.

This is not limited to nonfiction books and instructional videos, however. You can find occasional nuggets of information and inspiration in movies, music, video games, or any other form of entertainment that you consume during your leisure time.

I'll give you a couple of examples of times when I was unintentionally inspired while simply looking to be entertained.

In the 2006 Oscar-winning movie "The Departed," Jack Nicholson's character, Frank Costello, said something that snapped me out of passive-movie-viewer mode.

---

would go into a mild form of depression. Thankfully, those dark days are behind me. Now, I only read things that interest me.

I think those lines resonated especially deeply with me because of my race. I have a feeling that if I was any other ethnicity, those words might not have had the same impact. It took the concept of goal-setting to a completely different level for me. When I repeated that line to myself, it added an aggressiveness (which was lacking) to whatever I hoped to (legally) accomplish.

Another source of inspiration for me is 50 Cent's 2005 multi-platinum single, "In Da Club." You probably know this song – even if you think you don't. It's the one that goes:

"... go shawty,
It's your birthday
We gon' party like it's your birthday
We gon' sip Bacardi like it's your birthday..."

However, the section of the song that stood out the most to me was:

These lines made me realize that I needed to do something and be someone different, regardless of the naysayers, in order to make it to millionaire status.

In other words, it was up to me. No one else was going to do it for me.

UNDERSTANDING THE CULTURE OF MAKING MONEY

You may not think that making money is a way of life, but – like sports, Hollywood, religion, etc. – making money is definitely its own unique culture.

In my experience, nothing breaks down the walls of racism, sexism, homophobia, or any other bias or prejudice faster than the potential to make money – especially a lot of it. It is amazing to me what people can tolerate and/or overlook when making money is involved.

At times, many people have been hurt (both financially and emotionally) because they don't understand the customs of the culture. I liken it to someone dropping you in Pamplona, Spain, in the middle of bull-running season. Assuming you never saw the event on TV, you would be both figuratively and literally run over.

What are the customs of the money-making culture?

1) Making money is NEVER a charitable undertaking. Everyone is looking out for himself. You always have to protect your back. You are dealing with sharks (hence the name of the TV show "Shark Tank"). The most dangerous sharks are the ones who come off as personable and trustworthy. They make you lower your defenses, and when the time is right, they bite – stealing money from you, reneging on the original terms of a deal, or taking more of the equity for themselves. You may not want to become a shark, but **you must be able to recognize**

their behavior patterns. The only way to compete (or swim with the sharks) is to act as much like a shark as you can when discussing a potential money-making opportunity.

2) Learn to recognize when someone is slinging bullsh*t. Mind you, this type of bullsh*t is different than the type you grow intolerant of, as you get older. People who want or have a lot of money love to hear themselves talk. They'll say a lot of things that aren't true. This is the bullsh*t I'm referring to. It's not that they are intentionally lying to anyone, but they enjoy slinging bullsh*t. Bullsh*t usually means saying something that sounds pretty good but is highly unlikely to happen. Once you recognize the slinging of bullsh*t, feel free to sling some yourself. It's completely acceptable. I must caution you not to give or invest money in someone who is a bullsh*tter. You will lose your money, and the bullsh*tter will still feel the need to keep on slinging bullsh*t.
3) Don't confuse people respecting or liking *you* for people respecting and liking *the fact that you can make them money* or *the fact that you have money*. This is a common mistake and can lead to hurt feelings (primarily yours).
4) As long as money is being made or the potential to make money exists, people will be mostly agreeable unless egos need stroking.
5) Get everything in writing when money is concerned (i.e., contracts). People have a tendency to rewrite history or misremember conversations once the money starts (or stops) flowing.

6) Once money can no longer be made, don't be surprised if you lose touch with people you thought were your "friends." Those happy hours and steak dinners will vanish into thin air. Don't take it personally. People are always looking for the next money-making venture, and they're quick to move on when they sense that you can't help them make any more money.

CHAPTER 15

BE THANKFUL FOR THE A-HOLES IN YOUR LIFE

Everyone has to deal with a-holes.

Most people have varying degrees of tolerance for liars and cheaters, but very few can spend any considerable time around a true a-hole.

Mind you, a-holes come in as many varieties as Bubba Gump shrimp. There are racist a-holes, sexist a-holes, homophobic a-holes, religious a-holes, patronizing a-holes, sneaky a-holes, etc. And you can find a-holes just about everywhere: at work; at school; at the grocery store; at your church, synagogue, or mosque. You may even have an a-hole or two living under your own roof – sometimes, the biggest a-holes in our lives turn out to be our parents, siblings, or other family members.

I wish it were simple to look at someone and tell if they were an a-hole. That would save a lot of time and energy.

It's only through a person's words and/or actions that you gain a better sense of who they are. Most people put on a front when you first meet them, so you'll need to spend some time around a person before you can finally say with conviction: "*Wow, he's a real a-hole.*"[66]

I've learned that money is just a magnifier of a person's true self. Someone who is charitable will become more charitable (sometimes to a fault) if they come into a lot of money. Someone who is just a bit of an a-hole now will become a *major* a-hole if and when they ever make a tremendous sum of money.

Mind you, this is not the a-hole's fault. They may not be able to see themselves the way everyone else sees them. This is actually normal, and it makes sense, if you think about it: Who wakes up in the morning and thinks, "It's time to go out and be a complete a-hole!" Most a-holes lack self-awareness and empathy. And one byproduct of their becoming a millionaire is a (perhaps

66 I say "he" because in my millionaire journey, the people who seem to have the money, power, and control that I desired were usually males.

misaligned) sense of power and freedom. Possessing a lot of money has a way of making a-holes feel that they are somehow better or more deserving than the average person.

But your job is not to judge the a-holes or to determine their motivation for being a-holes. When you are dealing with an a-hole, your job is to use them as motivation to help you change your own life. A-holes force you to look deep within yourself to change your circumstances. They create adversity in your life and push you harder.

I wouldn't be where I am now if it weren't for the a-holes in my life. Every job, career decision, lifestyle choice – hell, even *this book* – was born out of my refusal for tolerating a-holes in my life any longer than absolutely necessary.

To paraphrase Horace, the Roman poet:

Adversity has the effect of eliciting talents, ideas, and dreams – which in agreeable, supportive, or pleasant circumstances would have lain dormant.

Even though I can be too intense for some people at times, I'm a pretty easygoing guy. I also pride myself on being extremely reasonable. I get along with 99% of the people I meet. And the 1% I don't get along with? These people used to piss me off, but now that I have gotten older and have a more mature perspective, I truly value and appreciate having these people in my life. Without their negative impact, I wouldn't have developed the intensity or desperation needed to escape from their influence or decisions.

Almost every story worth telling is, at its core, a story about a hero and an a-hole. It's the hero's mission to find a means to cope with or overcome the nefarious intentions of the a-hole.

The real world is very similar. On your journey to millionaire status, you will encounter a-holes who make your life difficult. But instead of hating them, appreciate them for providing the extra motivation you need to get where you're going.

Many successful people became successful, at least in part, thanks to an a-hole. Remember Bernie Marcus and Arthur Blank, the Home Depot guys from Chapter 5? They approached billionaire-turned-politician Ross Perot with their concept for a home improvement megastore, hoping that he'd like the idea enough to kick in a couple million dollars to help them get it off the ground. They wanted Perot's support badly enough that they were willing to offer him something like 70% ownership of the business. But Perot said no.

Now, does saying "no" make Perot an a-hole? No. But the *reason* he said no is a different story: Bernie drove a Cadillac. Perot was a Chevy man, through and through. Bernie's choice of car was the deal-breaker. Does that make Perot an a-hole? In my humble opinion: Hell, yes.

But things worked out for Bernie and Arthur. They started Home Depot without Perot's help, and they are now billionaires just like him. Bernie can afford to buy all the Cadillacs he wants, if Cadillacs are still his thing. Perot could have had a huge piece of that wealth, but he missed out because he wanted to be an a-hole about a car.

And who knows? Maybe if they'd gotten that $2 million from Perot, Bernie and Arthur wouldn't have felt the need to hustle as much as they did. Maybe they would have worked just a little less hard or put just a little less effort into the endeavor. Maybe Home Depot wouldn't have been as phenomenally successful as it is today. It's possible that, if Perot hadn't been so dead-set against Cadillacs, Home Depot might not be a household name.

It's like Horace said: Being comfortable or content doesn't force you into action. If you can't name one a-hole in your life, then you will have difficulty reaching your full potential. Dealing with a-holes day-in and day-out and trying to escape their influence in your life will stimulate your creative juices more than you can ever imagine.

My inner-city New York adolescence was full of a-holes - more than I could count. These were the people who wrote graffiti on freshly painted walls or treated the public staircases as their private urinals. Being surrounded by a-holes who didn't care enough to take care of their environment angered me very deeply. I hated that environment, and I couldn't wait to get out.

As I've gotten older, I've come to realize that, if I'd grown up in an environment that was more pleasant, I probably wouldn't have had such a strong desire for a change.

Before I leave this section, let me add one more thing. When you encounter an a-hole who brings adversity into your life, the most common emotion you will probably feel is anger. Anger is a very powerful motivator - if you know how to channel it properly. It's very tempting to criticize, cuss someone out, or get physical when you're very upset. A-holes who really piss you off make this temptation even greater. Unfortunately, these actions rarely produce long-term positive results. Remember the words of Michelangelo: *Criticize by creating.*

I admit that, in some cases, "criticize by creating" may not be enough. This is especially true in situations where you feel extremely pissed off or frustrated. In those situations, consider the words of Eleanor Roosevelt:

You must use that anger to propel your mind forward into the next evolution of your development. Anger, when channeled properly, will be the catalyst for your mind to elicit new talents, ideas, dreams, and opportunities.

NOW BOARDING, GROUP A(-HOLE)

Nearly every business or finance book to come out in the last two decades holds up Southwest Airlines as a shining example of innovation and company culture.

That might be true. But in my opinion, it's also the airline for a-holes.

If you are not familiar with or have never flown Southwest Airlines, it is unlike most airlines in that there is no assigned seating. They organize their passengers into 3 boarding groups: A, B, and C. The group you are in depends on when you check in for your flight. If you check in 24 hours early, you more than likely will be in the A group. If you check in 23 hours to 12 hours early, you'll probably be in the B group. And if you're one of the poor souls who checks in the morning of your flight or at the gate a couple of hours before, you're a C.

And when flying Southwest, you DO NOT want to be a C.

People in the A group get first dibs, and they can pretty much sit anywhere they want. The people in the B group don't have it that bad, though: They still have plenty of seating options after the A group gets settled.

The C group gets screwed. God help you as you try and find a seat. You'll be like little Forrest Gump, meandering down the school bus aisle, looking for a friendly face who will offer you a seat next to them. Every time I get on a crowded Southwest flight, there are always several people who occupy rows and block the middle seat so no one can sit there.

On one particular flight, I saw a guy (a real gold-star a-hole) who was sitting in an aisle seat take off his shoes and place them under the middle seat foot space. He then proceeded to place his computer (screen up and running) on the tray belonging to middle seat. To the not-so-observant passer-by, it would appear that someone must have been occupying that seat and probably just went to the restroom.

The lesson here? Sometimes, the A-holes win. They get the best seat on the plane, or they get the promotion you <u>believe</u> should have gone to you. Unfortunately, that's life. And life is not fair.

Don't let the battles distract you from the war – and don't let a few a-hole victories discourage you.

CHAPTER 16

KNOW WHEN TO SAY F*CK IT, PART 2

I've said it before, but I want to emphasize that your journey to millionaire status will not be easy. There will be setbacks and disappointments. You will probably fail at something at least once (but likely more than once). There will be moments when you may be so angry or you may feel so powerless and frustrated that you just feel like saying, "F*CK IT!"[67]

When you get to this point, you only have two options: Give up and accept that these are the cards life dealt you, OR get serious and decide that you're not putting up with this sh*t anymore. I choose to adopt the latter perspective, and I'd recommend that you do the same. This option will not only help you financially, but in other aspects of life as well. No one has the right to disrespect, mistreat, or undervalue you – and you shouldn't put up with it.

Now, keep in mind that you can't simply say "F*CK IT" any time things don't go your way. You aren't always going to get what you want, and sometimes (unless you're a toddler or you feel

67 We see the worst examples of this feeling in media coverage of things like mass shootings, terrorist attacks, and domestic murder-suicides. Behind every heinous act is a person (or a group of people) who reached a breaking point where they just said, "Ah, f**k it!"

extremely entitled) you just need to suck it up, accept things as they are, and keep moving forward. But there are times where "F*CK IT" is truly the only appropriate response.

So, how do you know if that situation is one you should tolerate or to which you should just say F*CK IT?

If you're not sure, ask yourself these four questions:

1) **Do you feel that you have not been or are not being treated fairly?**
2) **Have you tried communicating your viewpoints – on multiple occasions and in different ways?**
3) **Has the other party refused to listen or failed to take action?**
4) **Does the whole situation really just piss you off?**

If you can answer "Yes" to all four questions, guess what?

That's right: It's time to say F*CK IT.

But remember, after you choose to say "F*CK IT," ***you must channel that anger and frustration into becoming creative, not destructive***. Those who are prone to depression may choose to "escape" through alcohol, drugs, or suicide. Those who are more volatile may "go postal" and lash out physically at those around them.

As an INTJ, I tend to keep my emotions out of things. When I choose to say "F*CK IT," I do so in a calm, logical way – and only after I've come up with a plan. I know what I'm going to do next and how I'm going to do it.

If you know that you are someone who gets highly emotional in negative situations, you'll need to be prepared to manage the situation in a healthy, constructive way. Or as the late Viktor E. Frankl, author and Nazi concentration camp survivor, said:

I know... that's some deep sh*t, right?

Frankl was placed in the most horrible and hopeless of situations during the Holocaust, yet he maintained the mental and emotional fortitude to decide how he would respond to that situation. That mindset is what allowed him to persevere through the most challenging experience of his life.

The opposite of this mindset is "learned helplessness" – which is what happens when you feel that your circumstances are so challenging, so impossible, and so inescapable that you simply give up and resign yourself to the situation.

The example that comes to mind is an experiment conducted at the University of Pennsylvania in the 1960s. In the name of science, a group of psychologists placed a dog in a cage with an electrified floor. The psychologists (some real a-holes, if you ask me) would deliver a shock to the dog, who naturally would try to escape the pain of the shock by jumping to the other side of the cage. When he landed on the other side of the cage, another shock was waiting for him, so he would jump back to the original side – just to be shocked again. Initially, the dog would react by yelping, growling, or barking; sometimes the dog would urinate or defecate on himself. However, as the experiment went on and the dog realized that, no matter what he did, he would still get shocked, something very interesting, but also very sad, happened: The dog no longer responded to being shocked. It's not that he developed a tolerance to being shocked, and it wasn't that it was no longer was painful. But he knew that, no matter what he did, he couldn't escape. He was so conditioned into believing that he couldn't escape the pain that he no longer tried to escape – even when the researchers turned off the shock on the opposite side of the cage.

The dog believed that he couldn't change his situation, so he just lay there and took it.

What does this have to do with finance? A lot, actually! Because when challenging circumstances arise on your journey, you have two options: You can lie there like that dog, surrounded by piss and sh*t, and simply resign yourself to the situation. You can believe that there's nothing you can do; that this is how your financial life is always going to be. Or you can choose your response: Get mad, get fired up, and say F*CK IT.

I hope you choose the latter. I want you to say F*CK IT and start getting creative and strategic.

The key word here is "strategic": I AM NOT encouraging you to walk into your boss' office tomorrow morning and quit. You and your family may be dependent on the income your job provides. Plus, it's never a good idea to burn bridges that you have taken time to build.

If you've read to this point, you should have a good handle on your skills, your experience, and your intelligence type. You should have some idea of what the market believes you are worth. You should have a list of mentors you can turn to for inspiration.

And by now, who knows? Maybe you've started building up a decent side hustle.

My hope is that, in reading this book, you will be empowered and prepared to choose how you respond to a situation where you are being treated unfairly, undervalued, or pushed around by a bunch of a-holes. When you have a full understanding about your abilities, skills, and potential, you are in a far better position to say F*CK IT when necessary.

CHAPTER 17

RIGHT VS. WRONG NO LONGER MATTERS

If right and wrong were a color, they would be the muddiest of grays. Most of us have been programmed from childhood to always try to do the "right" thing – but this is something that you'll have to re-think as you continue your journey toward millionaire status.

So, if right and wrong no longer matter, what does?

Well, when it comes to making money, it all comes down to one question: Are your actions legal or illegal? Wealthy people are famous for bending the rules, but the majority of them will never break the law. In fact, many of them go as far as getting unfavorable laws changed (by hiring lobbyists) so that they can maximize the opportunity to profit from the system. And as long as they are abiding by the law, they will always be "right."

Let me give you an example: There have been several mass shootings across the U.S. in recent years. Some of these tragedies resulted in the deaths of innocent children. Collectively, many of us know that this is "wrong." After these types of tragedies occur, a passionate debate breaks out between those who believe we have a gun problem in America and those who are adamant that, "Guns don't kill people, people kill people."

At the end of the day, this conversation is a complete waste of time. A very serious issue gets lost in a verbal joust based on personal values. The ***ONLY*** thing that matters in this conversation is the law. In 1789, the forefathers of this great country wrote the following:

> ...the right of the people
> to keep and bear arms,
> shall not be infringed.
>
> 2nd Amendment
> United States Constitution

These 14 words, until changed by Congress, are the only thing that matter. It doesn't matter that, when the 2nd Amendment was written, semi-automatic and assault rifles were not yet in existence. I sometimes wonder: If the founding fathers could have foreseen the evolution in weapons technology, would they have crafted the law differently? I think so. It's obvious from other changes made to that original document that the founding fathers did not have all the answers. Since 1789, slavery has been abolished (13th amendment), slaves were granted citizenship (14th amendment), and black men and all women were granted the right to vote (15th and 19th amendments, respectively).

Let's also not forget that alcohol was made illegal (18th amendment) and then made legal again 16 years later (21st amendment).

Here are some examples of the actions that may be perceived as "wrong," but no laws were broken:

Steve Jobs, the late co-founder of Apple Inc., was paid $5,000 by Atari to develop a circuit board for a video game. Jobs, however, did not have the skill to complete the task on his own, so he got his friend (and subsequent Apple co-founder) Steve Wozniak to help him. He told Wozniak that Atari only gave him $700 and he would gladly split the money 50/50. Wozniak, being a trusting friend, agreed and completed the job as specified and on time. Jobs honored his commitment and paid Wozniak $350.

Did Jobs do something illegal? No. Was he an a-hole? Yes. But he didn't break any laws, so he technically didn't do anything "wrong."

Here's another example. Most parents teach their kids that fighting is wrong and not the best way to resolve problems. As an adult, if I were to get into a fight with someone, I could be arrested, charged with assault and battery, sued, and possibly end up in prison serving time.

However, if I decided to fight someone in boxing ring like Floyd "Money" Mayweather, Jr., I would be celebrated and potentially paid a ridiculous sum of money to pulverize my opponent. Fighting on the street equals getting in trouble, but fighting in the ring means potentially getting rich.

Why? Because the law is on my side.

I can't believe I'm getting paid $200 million to punch someone in the face as hard and as many times as I can.

As I write this book, there is a public outcry against Mylan, the pharmaceutical company responsible for manufacturing injectable epinephrine (better known as the EpiPen). This life-saving medication is used to treat severe allergic reactions – and when I say "severe," I mean severe: A person with a serious allergy could die in a matter of minutes if exposed to the wrong food, like nuts or shellfish, or if they get stung by a bee or a wasp.

In 2009, the EpiPen sold for $124. By 2016, and after 15 price hikes, the EpiPen is now priced at $609. If you don't know much about the pharmaceutical industry, you may believe that epinephrine is extremely difficult to produce in mass quantities. You're probably envisioning a group of scientists combing through the unknown perils of the Amazon jungle looking for the next epinephrine reservoir to save mankind against the threat of severe allergic reactions.

Let me tell you the truth: Epinephrine is cheap. It costs couple of dollars – at the most – to make it. What *isn't* cheap is retaining executive talent. While the wholesale price of the EpiPen rose by 400%, the CEO's salary rose by 600+%. According to an article on forbes.com by Emily Willingham, Mylan's CEO made $2.4 million in 2007. Eight years later, her total compensation (cash and stock) totaled almost $19 million. Mind you, she is not the only person to benefit from the EpiPen's price increase. Other executives and Mylan shareholders also benefited with a 200+% return on their investment in the company. You may have unknowingly benefited as well, if your 401k or mutual funds have any investments in the healthcare sector.

The public outcry about the price increase of this drug is understandable. How dare you put company, shareholder, and personal gain over the welfare of people's, particularly children's, health?

Because it's legal.

Here's another example of "right" vs. "wrong" not mattering: Donald Trump winning the 2016 election and becoming the 45th President of the United States. When he kicked off his campaign, I'm not sure anyone thought he could actually get elected. And during his campaign, many unfavorable things he said in the past were brought to the forefront. You may not like some of his so-called "locker room talk" about "grabbing women by the p*ssy." You may find it offensive when he calls Mexican immigrants criminals and rapists. You may object when he calls for a national "registry" of people who choose to follow a certain religion. But it doesn't matter if you like it or not. Nothing he said was illegal. Offensive maybe, wrong maybe, but not illegal.

You may not agree with the way Mylan does business. You may not believe that Donald Trump represents America. You can kick and scream all you want, but you can't change it. This is where you need to recite American theologian Reinhold Niebuhr's serenity prayer. For those of you who don't know it, here it is.

God,
Grant me the serenity
to accept the things
I cannot change
Courage to change the things I can
And the wisdom to know the
difference.

If you're an atheist, don't be turned off that the passage starts off with "God." Focus instead on the truth contained in the remainder of the passage. Those getting ahead in the world financially are those who may casually consider "right" vs. "wrong" in their decision-making but prefer to use the law as their moral compass.

I admit that this chapter will be very difficult to accept if you have a strong moral compass or lack any Machiavellian tendencies.

That said, I feel obligated to present all the tools you must use to become a millionaire. The world of making money is made up of people operating within the confines of the law but playing by their own rules. In America, 4% of the population consists of sociopaths – that's 1 in 25 people![68] These individuals can say or do anything without feeling the slightest degree of guilt, remorse, or shame. On the day consciences were being handed out, these people were unfortunately absent.

Like it or not, you'll need to break a few rules in order to get ahead in the world financially. And if we are really honest with ourselves, we all act like a-holes or mild sociopaths and break rules every now and then – especially if we are in a hurry, stressed, or pissed off.

Have you ever jumped into the grocery store's "12 Items or Less" line with 15 or 20 items in your basket? You know that you are breaking the "rules," but in the moment, getting out of the store faster is all you care about. The person at the register usually gives you a dirty look, and sometimes other customers will grumble or make snide comments.

You usually have three choices at this point:

1) Say something like, "Sorry! I didn't even see the sign!" Most people are not confrontational and will not want to escalate the conversation any further.
2) Ignore the cashier and/or other customers and stay put.
3) Go back to your original line.

If you opt for Choices 1 or 2, you can usually achieve the outcome you wanted (getting out of the store faster). If you opt for Choice 1, most people will stop grumbling and forgive you. They'll

68 This statistic comes from "The Sociopath Next Door" by Martha Stout, PhD, 2005.

probably remember a time when they, too, got in the wrong line or broke some minor rule. They'll forgive and forget, and everyone will move on.

The same kind of thing happens when a major corporation f*cks up in a really public way, whether it's releasing a product that hurts people or the environment; engaging in shady business practices; or fudging data to make their company seem more profitable, environmentally friendly, or successful. It's possible that it was an honest mistake - but it's just as likely that the company knew exactly what it was doing; it was cutting corners, jumping to the head of the line, and breaking rules just to get ahead and make as much money as quickly as possible.

It's a risk they're willing to take because they know that, as long as they're not doing anything illegal, most consumers will find it in their hearts to forgive and forget.

Comedian Emo Philips sums it up best:

I'm not sure if Judeo-Christian principles are at the root of our capacity to forgive people for the crappy things they do to us, or if it's just human nature.

Don't feel bad or guilty for acting in your best interests. This is not a license to be a complete a-hole, and I'm not advocating that you engage in malicious, hurtful behavior. But if you need to skip in line or break a few rules here and there, go for it. Everyone does it. And even if a few people get pissed off, they'll get over it fairly quickly.

FINAL NOTE

MONEY ISN'T EVERYTHING

Wait a minute. Isn't this is a book about becoming a millionaire?

Yes, that is correct. But I feel that I have to end the book with one very important note: Money isn't everything.

In fact, if you focus solely on making money, you may miss out on achieving higher levels of eventual success and wealth. And don't worry. I'm not going to mention anything about love or family. That's touchy-feely stuff. None of that will help you build wealth.

The one thing that will ALWAYS be more important than money (assuming you're in relatively good health) is TIME.

How many times have you thought, "If I only knew then what I know now"? As you enter middle or late adulthood, you will start to realize the importance of time. Money may be scarce, but time seems even scarcer. I have discovered that, although we may all be different, we are all equal in one way: Each of us only has 24 hours per day. Think about that for a minute. The richest people in the world can't use any of their money to buy more hours per day or quality years of life.

Time is truly life's ultimate equalizer.

Unfortunately, since most of us are not multi-millionaires or billionaires, we are often forced to trade our time in exchange for money. This is where you need to be careful. Don't trade away so much of your time working for others that you don't have any left over to spend on growing your skills. You can always make more money, but time spent is gone forever. Most employers do very little to develop new or additional skills in their employees. This is ultimately your responsibility.

Stay passionate.[69] Keep setting goals and building skills. And remember that time is the most valuable asset you own.

69 Notice that I didn't say, "Follow your passion." This is because, in most cases, following your passion may not help you become a millionaire. The phrase "starving artist" came about for a reason. If your goal is to become a millionaire, it's more important to develop your skills and set goals.

BONUS SECTION

HOW TO BECOME A SUPER-WEALTHY... POSSIBLY A BILLIONAIRE

The best coaches in every sport were never the best players. Great producers and directors were never the best actors or performers. So, just because I'm not a billionaire, doesn't mean I can't help you fulfill your potential.

For this exercise to work, you must imagine that I am your coach. I may not have the skill to do it myself, but my job is *not* to dunk the ball, throw the touchdown, or write the computer program. Rather, my role is to help you understand how you can maximize your economic potential.

If you want to become a billionaire, you and your network must possess a skill AND have direct ownership of products or services that touch and/or impact many peoples' lives (whether they are aware of it or not).

A quick test to figure out how many peoples' lives you impact is:

1) Do you produce a product or deliver a service that has the potential to affect multiple (at least 1 million) lives

simultaneously and consistently?

2) Does the impact of your work or your investments have the potential to be felt nationally or globally?

3) How much money do you have in your control? How many people, institutions, or governments would be willing to give you money to manage on their behalf? Can you allocate that capital to generate above-average returns?

If you have developed your skills to this level, you definitely have billionaire potential. I encourage you to go after your dreams.

Drop me a line and let me know if you make it.

AFTERWORD

I hope that this book has inspired you to pursue your financial dreams and that you feel a little bit energized or fired up after reading it.

It's not easy to become a millionaire. It requires a lot of hard work, and – depending on factors like your race, gender, and religion; your education level; your financial background; and your geographical location – the odds may not be in your favor.

But I hope that you realize that it's not impossible to become a millionaire, no matter who you are or where you come from. I hope that, as you come to these final pages, you think:

If Paul Alleyne – a black guy from a barely middle class, inner-city, single-parent family – did it...

WHY CAN'T I?
WHY NOT ME?

This book is solely focused on the practical steps you need to take in order to become a millionaire. I think it would be irresponsible for me not to offer a few words of non-monetary insight.

These are probably things you have already heard before, but they're worth repeating. Here goes:

Money won't make you happy.
Money won't change you, but rather magnify your current self.

Along my journey of building wealth, I have learned that people have vastly different values and senses of morality, particularly when it comes to money. I may have helped you become wealthier, but it's your responsibility to make sure that you build a life that is worth living and – more importantly – fulfilling (based on your own values) because you can't take any of your sh*t with you when you eventually kick the bucket.

A Pablo Picasso quote best represents this for me and will be my final words to you:

RECOMMENDED RESOURCES

Books
(in no particular order)

1) "Mindset: The New Psychology of Success" by Carol Dweck
2) "The Jewish Phenomenon: Seven Keys to the Enduring Wealth of a People" by Steven Silbiger
3) "The Triple Package: How Three Unlikely Traits Explain the Rise and Fall of Cultural Groups in America" by Amy Chua and Jed Rubenfeld
4) "The 50th Law" by 50 Cent and Robert Greene
5) "How Successful People Think" by John Maxwell
6) "Start With Why: How Great Leaders Inspire Everyone to Take Action" by Simon Sinek
7) "No Excuses!: The Power of Self-Discipline" by Brian Tracy
8) "Seven Habits of Highly Effective People" by Stephen Covey
9) "Quiet: The Power of Introverts in a World That Can't Stop Talking" by Susan Cain

Apps

1) Franklin Covey: Living the 7 Habits
2) Entrepreneur Daily by Entrepreneur Media

ILLUSTRATION CREDITS

The illustrations in this book were drawn by Daniela Weil, based on the following images:

Page 4 Stephen Covey, stephencovey,com
Page 8 Morpheus Paul, The Matrix, Warner Bros.
Page 11 Sisyphus, Sisyphusa by Michael Richmond cover art
Page 20 Bob Marley, Legend album cover, Island Records
Page 22 Mental Shackle Images inspired by The Mis-Education of the Negro by Carter G. Woodson cover art, Africa World Press 1990
Page 28 Robert Herjavec, robertherjavec.com
Page 40 Lil Jon, Get Low Lil Jon, tumblr.com
Page 41 JJ Watt, Sporting News
Page 66 Lin Manuel Miranda, Joan Marcus
Page 68 Michelangelo, Michelangelo Biography, biography.com, A&E Television Networks
Page 75 Latrell Sprewell, top5.com
Page 86 Warren Buffett, Getty Images
Page 119 John Wooden, The Associated Press
Page 140 Tim McGraw, Live Like You Were Dying album cover, Curb Records
Page 147 Socrates, Socrates Mind Map, tes.com
Page 165 Jack Nicholson, The Departed, Warner Bros. / Everett
Page 166 50 Cent, 50 Cent Bio, rollingstone.com

Page 172 Forrest Gump, Forrest Gump, Paramount Pictures / Everett
Page 173 Horace, crystalinks.com
Page 176 Eleanor Roosevelt, America's First Ladies, C-SPAN
Page 181 Viktor Frankl, charterforcompassion.org
Page 188 Floyd Mayweather Jr., The Source
Page 190 Reinhold Niebuhr, AP Photo, File
Page 192 Emo Philips, A Moment in Time From My "Cinemax Comedy Experiment", emophilips.com
Page 200 Pablo Picasso, Pablo Picasso Biography, biography.com, A&E Television Networks

ACKNOWLEDGEMENTS

The idea for this book was born summer 2015, and the finished work you now hold in your hands took almost two years to complete. It is the result of hard work, dedication, and allowing myself to ask for help and guidance from those who have traveled the path before me. This is not a sign of weakness, but rather wisdom, in my opinion. If I may paraphrase a popular African proverb based on what this experience has taught me: "It takes a village to write and publish a book."

First, I would like to thank my editors Stephanie Hashagen, Wintress Odom, and Erin Larson from The Writers for Hire in Houston, Texas for making my message clearer, bolder, and more in-your-face (i.e. upping the F-bomb count). Next, I would like to thank my illustrator, Daniela Weil, who brought the images in my mind to life and kept her promise to show no mercy if she thought my writing sucked. And finally, I would like to thank the many people I've met in my life's journey; people who have lived with so much passion that I felt an overwhelming need to look deep within myself and say:

F*CK IT. I'M FINALLY GOING TO WRITE THIS BOOK.

CPSIA information can be obtained
at www.ICGtesting.com
Printed in the USA
BVHW081028121221
623851BV00005B/529